BRIDGING BOUNDARIES:

THE PASTORAL CARE
OF U.S. HISPANICS

BRIDGING BOUNDARIES:

THE PASTORAL CARE
OF U.S. HISPANICS

Edited by:

Kenneth G. Davis and Yolanda Tarango

Scranton: University of Scranton Press

Library of Congress Cataloging-In-Publication Data

Bridging Boundaries : the pastoral care of U.S. Hispanics / edited
by Kenneth G. Davis and Yolanda Tarango.
    p. cm.
    Includes bibliographical references (p.) and index..
    ISBN 0-940866-81-1 – ISBN 0-940866-82-X
    1. Church work with Hispanic Americans. 2. Hispanic American
    Catholics–Religion.
    I. Davis, Kenneth G., 1957- II. Tarango, Yolanda.

BX1407.H55 B75 1999
282'.73'08968–dc21

                                                    99-048866

Disbribution:
University of Toronto Press
2250 Military Road
Tonawanda   NY   14150
1-800-565-9523

CONTENTS

ACKNOWLEDGMENTS

The chapters by Fernández, Tabares, Boran, and my chapter titled "Original Fervor": A New Catholic Reformation? were previously published in December 1997 in *Chicago Studies* (volume 36, number 3). They appear here with permission. My introduction draws on matter from my article in *Listening: A Journal of Religion and Culture*, which appeared in Fall 1997 (volume 32, number 3). It too is printed with permission. We are grateful to these two journals both for originally printing these timely essays and for allowing us to use them in this book. "Still Gringo After All These Years" first appeared in *Quarterly Review: A Journal of Theological Resources for Ministry. Apuntes: Reflexiones Teológicas Desde El Margin Hispano* originally printed the essay on Central Americans. And the final chapter of this work was first published in *The Journal of Hispanic/Latino Theology* (1) 3 May 1994: 68–79. Please note, however, that each reprinted essay has been modified (e.g., explanatory notes removed) and updated. Readers may wish to consult the originals.

Consultants included Allan F. Deck, S.J. and Virgil Elizondo. María Garcia helped with the bibliography. Its brevity attests to the need of a work such as this one. Proofreaders were David Black and John Voca, O.F.M., CONV. All five deserve our thanks. We wish to acknowledge the kind assistance of Anthony Stevens-Arroyo and the Office of Research for Religion in Society and Culture at Brooklyn College of the City University of New York. We are especially grateful to Ada María Isasi-Díaz for her perceptive preface.

PREFACE

Ada María Isasi-Díaz

The emphasis that emerged from Vatican II on the church as the People of God turned our attention from an almost exclusive importance on sacramental ministry to a focus on pastoral ministry. Hand in hand with this new understanding of the church, Vatican II affirmed the importance of incarnating the gospel message in the culture of the various peoples who had embraced the teaching of Jesus. This book focuses on these two priorities of the Catholic Church and offers understandings and guidelines that will help those who minister to Hispanics. Repeatedly the articles in this book make it very clear that, since Hispanics will soon be 50% of the Catholic Church in the USA, the institutional church would do well to value the religious understandings and practices of Hispanic Catholics and minister with us accordingly.

Two elements need to be analyzed here. The first is a theological one grounded in the ancient church teaching that of the *sensus fidelium*. This sense of the faithful means that the revelation of God continues over the ages in the midst of the people of God, a revelation that Hispanics see expressed in a very specific way in our *religión popular* (popular religion). It is thanks to *religión popular* that Christianity is a vital force in many families and communities, serving not only as the principal tool for catechizing, but also as the vehicle for ministry among Hispanics. Unfortunately, while the institutional church is far from recognizing this phenomenon, it continues to look for ways to baptize *religión popular*. For instance, many official church ministers utilize *religión popular* to attract Hispanics to church functions instead of valuing it as a true expression of the people's belief and committed Christian living. This disregard of Hispanic *religión popular* is devastating to our culture within USA society, a society which most of us experience as dominant and oppressive. Surveys and studies through the last four decades have repeatedly shown that one of the key elements of Hispanic identity is religion, religion as manifested in *religión popular* and not necessarily church affiliation and participation. The maintenance of a Hispanic identity is considered by many of us to be key in our ability to survive in an alien land alien because of our different culture, not necessarily because of geography. (After all, this land is the homeland of a vast number of the largest groups of Hispanics: the Mexican-Americans.) So *religión popular* plays a double role: it is a vehicle of and for the Christian faith in Hispanic communities, and it is a liberative praxis in the sense that it helps us to hold on to one of the key elements of our Hispanic identity: the Christian religion.

The second element that needs to be understood in a new way is that of diversity. Though Native Americans, of course, were in this land first, we Hispanics were here before any other group of immigrants. Thus we stand fully in the American tradition of being a nation of immigrants. But the diversity of Hispanics has to be dealt with differently from the way the diversity of past waves of immigrants was handled. Why? Great differences exist between the reasons why immigrants came here at the turn of last century and throughout the first half of the century now ending and the reasons why Hispanic immigrants come today. Simply put, there are many differences between the world of European immigrants and the Latin American and Caribbean worlds of Hispanics. First, there is the role that the USA has played in creating or allowing the political and/or economic conditions in our countries of origin that have forced many of us to immigrate to the USA. Then there is the fact that geographic proximity and modern means of transportation and communication keep Hispanics' ties with our countries of origin very strong: we often travel to our countries of origin and continuous waves of immigrants from Latin American and the Caribbean are always renewing those ties. Further, there is the fact that, because of the prevalent racism of this society, only certain kinds of immigrants have been permitted to contribute to what it means to be a USA citizen, to be an American. Clearly African Americans have never been included as an element of the melting pot and neither have Native Americans, Asian Americans, nor Hispanics. All of these factors indicate that unless a different understanding of diversity comes into play in this country, the USA will succumb to even more prejudice and discrimination.

Diversity has to be understood in a non-essentialist way. Differences do not necessarily entail contradiction or exclusion. In most differences there are some elements of sameness or likeness, *iguales o por lo menos parecidos*. It is precisely those elements of sameness or likeness that make dialogue possible and that enrich a people, a nation, a church. For this enrichment to happen, however, not only must the diversity be recognized as non-essentialist but it must also be valued. And this is the challenge that Hispanics present to the Catholic Church and other churches in this country. We are different and we ask those in charge of the churches and society to understand those differences as non-exclusionary or contradictory to their own identity or to the institutions they serve. We also ask, particularly of our church leaders, that they recognize the ongoing revelation of God in our midst, and see the differences in our way of being Catholic, *en nuestra manera de ser católicas y católicos*. It is a source of enrichment, an important element for the revitalization of our faith and of the whole church in the USA.

Only when our way of being Catholic is seen as enriching will the church be able to minister effectively with Hispanics. Only when diversity is truly embraced will the institutional church become a key element of Hispanic culture in the USA the same way the Christian faith, through the expressions of *religión popular*, has been essential since the beginnings of our *mestizo* and *mulato* cultures. This is what the pastoral agents who have contributed to this book say repeatedly. Their observations grow out of their pastoral practice with the Hispanic community. This volume should be food for thought for all those involved in ministry with Hispanics. Furthermore, the under-standings contained in this book and even the suggestions here articulated only in an incipient way should have much to contribute to parish and diocesan pastoral plans, even national Hispanic pastoral plans. Only then will the church be able to grow in wisdom and in grace as Jesus did; only then will the church be able to incarnate that intrinsic element of the gospel message: the commandment to act justly.

INTRODUCTION

Kenneth G. Davis, O.F.M., Conv.

One of my former college professors told me that the title of this book is a mixed metaphor. He was disappointed with my delight. However, what better way to illustrate the situation of the *mestizo, mulato, ladino, criollo*, the alchemy that is the one common element of all U.S. Latinos and Latinas? We use "bridge" as a verb since we are trying to show connections between the distinct elements of this mixture inherent in Hispanicity without either ignoring those differences or accepting dichotomies. Hispanics are the catalyst of the alchemy necessary to Christian charity precisely because they embrace the differences that often divide other communities. There are boundaries that distinguish them without becoming fissures that divide them. They are the *raza cósmica*, the cosmic race, that group which embraces the bloodlines of virtually every continent. We identify and seek to bridge six of these boundaries.

Culture is the first border bridged in this volume about cross-boundary ministry. I touch upon it in my introductory essay and again in "Still Gringo After All These Years." All ministry among Hispanics in the United States is cross-boundary. Borders that must be negotiated are not just cultural or geographic, however. Very often Latinos and Latinas of one group (e.g., Cubans) work with Hispanics of a different group (e.g., Puerto Ricans). The second boundary they must negotiate is ethnicity. In this volume we include chapters on Hispanic groups about whom comparatively little has been written, specifically Dominicans, South Americans, and Central Americans.

Third, even when the ethnic background of the minister and the parish is the same, differences in levels of acculturation are boundaries between them. For example, they must bridge differences of language between immigrants and their children born in the United States. Both George Boran and Eduardo Fernández build these bridges.

Fourth are sexual boundaries. Every culture distinguishes between gender roles. This boundary between Latinos and Latinas is manifested uniquely. Both Yolanda Tarango and Ada María Isasi-Díaz are pioneers in the area of gender distinctions among Hispanics. They and Irma S. Corretjer-Nolla clarify the distinctions and build the bridges we seek.

Fifth are racial boundaries. Hispanics may be of any race. The chapters by Anneris Goris and Adele González are among the few publications that describe race relations among Hispanics of distinct or mixed race.

Finally, there are religious as well as denominational boundaries. Formal church structures and authorities may never touch those who celebrate popular rituals and domestic prayer. In the last chapter I deal with this continuum of religious experience.

Given these six boundaries and the need to bridge without obliterating them, a minister in this context must evolve into a kind of amphibian. Ministers are never complete insiders to the community across the boundary, yet they also never again relate in the same way to their home culture after crossing those boundaries. Cross-boundary ministers always inhabit an in-between place of ambiguity and tension, potential and promise: That is the incongruous position of a bridge. It can only connect distinct places by maintaining its place between them.

An example of the cross-boundary minister to which I refer is the Apostle Paul. As were many Christians of later centuries, Saul was a zealous adherent to his religious tradition and a firm believer in this inviolate boundary. He sincerely thought that God had mandated his fierce crusade. Just as many nineteenth century missionaries participated in the conquest and colonization of territories formerly of Spain and Mexico, so Saul oppressed other persons with the blessing of his own religious superiors.

What a shock then when Christ called his religious vocation "persecution." He was knocked down and blinded by this realization. Recall that his companions heard the voice, but their response was very different. It is not easy to be shocked out of boundaries firmly held, blessed by religion, and supported by friends and family. Such boundaries help construct and maintain self-identity.

How did Saul recover his shattered self and regain his sight? He had to cross boundaries; he had to seek out and live with a member of the community he had formerly hated and threatened: Ananias. Ananias was not naive; he knew Saul's reputation as an adversary. But Ananias followed God's will. He took in his former foe, prayed with him, baptized him, and introduced him to the community at Damascus. This solidarity with the oppressed and their loving forgiveness of his former persecution opened Saul to healing and the beginning of his renewed identity. Communication, prayer, and forgiveness bridged the boundaries of culture and religion.

Unfortunately, suspicion of the newly converted Saul did not end. The disciples in Jerusalem wanted nothing to do with him. Throughout the rest of his life Saul, now Paul, struggled with misunderstanding from every quarter. The Pharisees, the community to which he had belonged, rejected and persecuted him. Does not the virtual silence concerning his family speak volumes about the cost he paid to cross geographic, religious, and cultural boundaries? The silence of Paul's family and his sometimes tumultuous relationship with the young John Mark show that Paul also had to bridge both generational and familial boundaries.

At the same time, his new community, the Christians, continuously vexed him. He was never completely accepted either by Christian or Jew; he was a *mestizo*, someone in-between worlds that are parallel yet distinct. All his ministry occurred on this frontier, on the border, simultaneously negotiating many boundaries. This is the world of United States Hispanic ministry.

Did Paul reject his Jewishness? The realization that God had not supported the presumed superiority of his previous vocation threatened his former identity. Boundaries he had accepted split open like fissures. Yet he did not hate himself or seek to reject his roots. He neither ignored these boundaries nor sought to obliterate them. He bridged them by reinterpreting his own identity. He did not reject his faith tradition but allowed it to be reinterpreted and completed in Christ. He bridged boundaries, living among the Gentiles, much like a Greek, without ever casting off his Jewish culture. This was not the negation of his home, but a renewed understanding of it, based on a reflective experience of God who always exists on both sides of every border.

Because of his past, Paul called himself the least of the apostles; but he also insisted on the role God had chosen for him. Paul was the apostle to the Other, the Gentile. Because he was the greatest apostolic cross-cultural minister, he is the model missionary. He represents a minister able to cross religious, geographic, cultural, generational, linguistic, and even gender boundaries (see Florence Morgan Gillman's *Women Who Knew Paul*. Collegeville, MN: The Liturgical Press, 1992). Though never Pontifex, he was a bridge builder.

Cyprian Davis, O.S.B., claims that there are only two integrated institutions in the United States: the military and the Catholic Church. This is a great but often unpublicized truth. However, it is also true that integration does not always mean equality. An integrated institution requires leaders who understand and love their own home culture, but who can also criticize it in the light of the Gospel. We need leaders who can build bridges that connect the many boundaries.

This book, which celebrates the diversity of U.S. Hispanic ministry, suggests how we might bridge boundaries of culture, generation, ethnicity, language and acculturation, gender, race, and religion. The first chapter provides the context for U.S. Hispanic ministry and touches upon the various boundaries that intersect there. The final chapter directly addresses the religious boundaries among various denominations and between popular and official Catholic worship. George Boran's discussion of Hispanic Catholic youth in the United States contends that Latinos comprise our country's youngest ethnic group. Yet only about 5% of them are involved in formal church structures. Boran suggests some specifics on bridging this gap. Eduardo C. Fernández shows how working with Chicanos can uncover an ancient Christian intuition. Both chapters cross boundaries of generation and acculturation. Fanny Tabares encourages the church to work for a world where there are no barriers of race, culture, or language. Like my chapter on Central Americans, Tabares distinguishes between various Hispanic groups not by creating blocks, but by dialoging with differences. Irma S. Corretjer-Nolla addresses gender in her essay on Puerto Rican women. Adele González remembers the Mariel boatlift, and Anneris Goris outlines pastoral care to Dominicans. In these two chapters boundaries of race are bridged and become stepping stones to communion.

And this brings us to the dedication of this book. Las Hermanas is a group of women long dedicated to bridging boundaries and removing stumbling blocks. To these bridge builders we dedicate this volume with our thanks.

"ORIGINAL FERVOR": A NEW CATHOLIC REFORMATION?

Kenneth G. Davis, O.F.M., Conv.

As I look to a renewal or new reformation of our church, I recall the words of Junípero Serra, one of the first evangelizers of the United States. In the last letter before his death he wrote words as applicable today as when this ministry began.

> May God grant you the graces necessary for the right training and development of our new missionaries! May they not be like the old ones; the more one gave into them, the more they redoubled their demands! . . . Now that you are few in number, that the lesson of the dead is still present to all, that there have been so many desertions, and that a new era is beginning . . . would this not be the moment to revive the original fervor? (Englebert, Omar. *The Last of the Conquistadores: Junípero Serra.* New York: Harcourt, Brace and Co., 1956)

This first chapter provides context for current United States Hispanic ministry. It is the buttress of the bridges the other chapters build. While, as in the eighteenth century, one can also doubt our ministers today, grieve the dead, mourn those who have left the ministry, and complain about abuses, the saints among us constantly recall our "original fervor." Mine began decades ago.

I attended a public high school in Kentucky. A neighbor boy also attended, and sat next to me during lunch. One day he asked about the Jerusalem cross I was wearing. When I explained that I was a Catholic, he rose in a huff, snatched away his tray and hissed, "Hell, I can't sit with you, I'm a Christian!"

What's in a name? Much, especially if one is in the minority, as I was in that school. Others called us "papists," "mackerel snappers," or "lovers of the Whore of Babylon." Those were scarlet letters that obscured rather than revealed.

The appellation "Hispanic" similarly obscures rather than reveals. It is an umbrella term that the Census Bureau invented once they finally attended to the population so described. It refers to persons living in the United States who trace their heritage to a combination of Spanish, African, or Native American ancestry. Many scholars prefer the name "Latino," while others reject any universal term and insist on more precise descriptions, for instance, "Puerto Rican." It is essential to understand the diversity within the community generally called "Hispanic."

Some twenty-seven million Hispanics live in the United States, comprising about 10% of the population. This segment of the country is growing quite rapidly. Its average age is approximately ten years younger than that of European Americans such as myself. Around 60% are of Mexican descent, 14% are Puerto Rican, and 5% Cuban. The rest come from at least twelve other countries, giving the United States the fifth largest Spanish-speaking population of any nation on the globe.

Hispanics are a highly urbanized group, but are no longer found only in five or six states. "From 1980 to 1992, the number of Hispanics in the 10 Midwest states . . . climbed from 1.2 million to 1.8 million. Over the same period, the white population in those states declined by 400,000" (Debbie Howlett, "Midwest New Hub for Hispanics," *USA Today*, 15 December 1995).

Many Hispanics are professionals or entrepreneurs, but as a whole, the group is poor. Many other common assumptions prove to be erroneous in the face of these facts: 1) More than 60% were born in the United States 2) More than 70% are bilingual. 3) While not primarily agricultural workers, they are very mobile. 4) They are less than half as likely as Euro-Americans or Asian Americans to use welfare. 5) They smoke, drink, and use drugs less than Euro-Americans or African Americans. 6) They have a very low divorce rate. 7) They have a very strong work ethic (United States Department of Commerce, *Hispanic Americans Today*. Washington: Bureau of the Census, 1993).

Moreover, they are quite orthodox in their views of Catholicism and not necessarily less likely to practice the faith (Gilbert R. Cadena, "Religious Ethnic Identity: A Socio-Religious Portrait of Latinas and Latinos in the Catholic Church," in Stevens-Arroyo, Anthony and Gilbert R. Cadena, *Old Masks, New Faces: Religion and Latino Identities*. New York: The Bildner Center, 1995).

Hispanics were the first Catholics to arrive in what is now the United States. Nearly all of the oldest church buildings in the country, the Franciscan missions, were built by them. Today they make up approximately 30% of the total United States Catholic population. Within a decade they could easily be the majority. This projection, however, depends to a great degree on whether they will continue to be attracted to other denominations.

Why Are They Leaving the Church?

Perhaps Hispanics are attracted to denominations in which they more easily enter positions of leadership, feel greater ownership, and therefore feel more welcome.

They have little influence in the Catholic Church in the United States. Fewer than 5% of our bishops are Hispanic. Similarly, fewer than 5% of the priests, religious or degreed lay leaders, are Hispanic (Felician A. Foy and Rose M. Avato, eds., *The Catholic Almanac.* Huntington, IN: Our Sunday Visitor Press, 1995. Marie Augusta Neal, SND., "American Sisters: Organizational and Value Changes," in David G. Bromley and Helen Rose Ebaugh, eds., *Religion and Social Order: Vatican II and United States Catholicism.* Greenwich, CT: JAI Press, Inc., 1991). Of the nation's permanent deacons, fewer than 13% are Latinos (*CARA Report*, Fall 1995). The Winter 1998 *CARA Report* states that "Hispanic/Latino students make up 11 percent of graduate-level seminarians, 16 percent of those in diaconate formation, and 24 percent of people in lay ministry formation programs." This situation is also complicated by other factors.

First, as a study by Edwin Hernández et al., shows, some 70% of Catholics ministering to this population are not themselves Hispanics. There is overwhelming and repeated data showing that we European Americans, with few exceptions and despite the best intentions, are often ineffective and sometimes counterproductive in this ministry (Díaz-Stevens, Ana María and Anthony M. Stevens-Arroyo. *Recognizing the Latino Resurgence in United States Religion: The Emmaus Paradigm.* Boulder, CO: Westview Press, 1998).

This situation will not change soon, considering that Protestant seminarians of Hispanic background currently outnumber Catholic Hispanic seminarians three to one. Very few Catholic Church leaders are given adequate cross-cultural training, and many are not even aware of the need.

This lack of native leadership leads to a host of problems and is probably one reason for the massive shift of formerly Catholic Hispanics to Pentecostal, Evangelical, and other Protestant denominations. Nearly all of these denominations have a polity that allows Hispanics much more opportunity for leadership in their churches.

Virgilio Elizondo sees a parallel between the model of leadership found in these denominations and the experience of apparitions in the Catholic tradition. In both instances, ordinary people with no ecclesial office or authorization claim to receive communications from the Holy. These ordinary people begin to make public testimony to the experience and rapidly find a following. Initially there is often opposition from the local clergy. The parallel breaks down, of course, since some visionaries, such as Saint Bernadette, submit to church authority and others do not perceive a need to do so.

However, in less dramatic ways, leadership among Catholic Hispanics usually follows this course. Since there have never been enough clergy to serve the Hispanic population, confraternities and sodalities have maintained buildings and sponsored feasts. Rituals that do not require clergy, such as the Way of the Cross, became popular. Mothers and grandmothers catechized in informal ways. Ordinary people, inspired by a simple faith, testifying to their beliefs through home devotions and public rituals, have historically exercised Hispanic church leadership. This pattern of home-grown leadership worked well in pre-modern rural environments. Unfortunately, it very often met with misunderstanding and even hostility when non-Hispanic clergy moved into the newly conquered Southwest in the mid-nineteenth century, or into Puerto Rico fifty years later.

This long and unfortunate struggle between native Hispanic leadership and ignorant, sometimes insensitive non-Hispanic clergy and other ecclesial leaders continues today. Unlike European immigrants, Hispanics do not have numerous native clergy to champion them. Unlike Europeans, they did not originally choose to emigrate; their territory was conquered. When the United States church appears to support the values of the conqueror, when there is no recognized leadership to safeguard the rightful place of the Hispanic in the Catholic Church, Latinos feel unwelcome.

If a Christian (often Hispanic) from another denomination knocks on the door of Latinos who feel unwelcome in the Catholic Church, and not only invites them into a small, welcoming community but encourages them to take ownership and leadership, they respond enthusiastically. They need not leave their community for a strange seminary, overcome educational obstacles, or endure prejudice. Like the children of Fátima, they feel they are accepted as they are, and are allowed to contribute their testimony.

This does not mean they are children. Quite the opposite. It means their rich spiritual heritage sometimes clashes with certain aspects of mainstream United States Catholicism. Sometimes resistance to this living critique, older and often more authentically Catholic than that which it critiques, is so strong that a mature Hispanic adult feels it too much to bear.

Not a Hispanic Problem But a Catholic Challenge

Twenty years ago, some 85% of United States Hispanics identified themselves as Catholic; today this figure is around 65%. This is the largest loss of Catholics since the sixteenth century. Yet we hold no Council (of Trent) and establish no new religious communities (of Jesuits) in response. Indeed we have done little more than complain and publish position papers. Andrew Greeley is only the best known and most recent sociologist to call this "an ecclesiastical failure of unprecedented proportions." Ronaldo Cruz, executive director of the NCCB Secretariat for Hispanic Affairs, has said that we repeatedly fail to put our resources into making our paper positions palpable.

I am not only concerned with this numerical loss, however. I am even more disturbed by the loss of this oldest Christian spirituality native to America. Hispanics are the most ancient Catholic community in the United States. They are by far the largest and probably still the strongest of the "cultural Catholic" groups.

Therefore, the question is not only important to Hispanics. If the church were an ecosystem, and an ancient and vibrant species were fleeing in great numbers, one would look to a flaw within the environment. It seems to me that we must ask: What does this mass exodus mean for the whole United States church? To what extent is it due to prejudice? Do we truly encourage lay leadership? How are we opening Catholic schools, seminaries, and chanceries to what the United States bishops have called the Hispanic gift and blessing?

As a Franciscan, I find this particularly troublesome. My community evangelized the Americas and helped to forge this *mestizo* (mixed-race) Christianity. One of the finest moments in the order's history was the mission of the "twelve apostles" sent to Mexico. The earliest friars studied the native languages and cultures (some consider them the first anthropologists), defended the natives before the Spanish throne, and heroically sacrificed themselves in an evangelization effort that, although not perfect nor wholly successful, was perhaps unprecedented.

Compare the history of the spread of the gospel west from the original thirteen American colonies to the history of its spread south through Mexico and South America. The United States has few Native Americans, and fewer of these who know their own language and culture. But in Mexico, Central and South America, there are millions of indigenous people who have maintained their cultural and linguistic heritage. This is partly attributable to the all too imperfect efforts to evangelize the indigenous peoples of the south. In the north, deliberate eradication was more common than conscious evangelization.

That is why we still see the stamp of mendicant spirituality even today in Hispanic popular rites. This United States Hispanic school of spirituality "is not found in any book, rule or structure but rather in the daily life encounters" (Pérez, Arturo, and Consuelo Cuvarrubias with Edward Foley, *Así Es: Stories of Hispanic Spirituality*. Collegeville, MN: The Liturgical Press, 1994). Those encounters include Christmas plays or *pastorelas* and the dedication to the Passion of Jesus shown by the *penitentes*. They include the *posadas* of Augustinian origin and the many eloquent plays or dances such as the Jesuit-inspired *matachines*.

These are only a few examples of the melding of the Christian message with indigenous spirituality. From this forge emerged the most ancient and perhaps the sturdiest expression of Catholicism known to the United States.

Some of the greatest Catholic saints suffered and many died to bring the gospel of Christ to the Americas. Perhaps the most precious fruit of this flawed yet noble attempt is the Catholicity and unique devotional expressions of the Latino peoples. Since the middle of the past century, these heirs of the trailblazers of Christianity on the continent have been incorporated (sometimes through conquest) into the United States church.

Does not our church, living on the cusp of the next century, owe a debt to our *antepasados* (ancestors)? Will history remember us as champions of a great if imperfectly realized cause like *los doce* (the twelve), the first friars in Mexico, or shall we be mute witnesses to the dismantling of their heroism and the loss of a culture once so thoroughly Catholic?

A Challenge and Opportunity

Gary Riebe-Estrella, S.D.V., wrote:

My hypothesis is that United States Catholics of European descent, generally speaking, in moving into the center of United States society, have taken on the national ethos and that their attitudes toward Latinos do not differ in the main from those of the general population.

As a Catholic of European descent, I must agree. I accept this challenge for a new counter-reformation. By this I mean a counter-cultural reformation: a renewal of the Catholic Church in the United States through, among other things, valuing and promoting that spirituality, which is perhaps the most pristine precisely because it never entered the mainstream United States culture. United States Hispanic spirituality is a resource for a counter-cultural reformation of the whole church.

Marcello Azevedo, S.J., sees the blessing of this cross. Hispanics are twice foreign. They are foreign in this country because the majority is Protestant. They are foreign secondly because they are a minority in their own Catholic Church. However, this is also their privilege.

Not only do they serve as a bicultural and bilingual bridge between the churches of the Americas, but also their socio-cultural singularity has helped them resist certain aspects of United States cultural Catholicism. That is why they are in a privileged position to help critique and transform those values of North American culture that are contrary to Catholic thought and practice.

Therefore, I do not see their presence as a threat to my culture; I see their presence as an aid to my faith. I do not see their critique as a problem but a challenge I am happy to take up. And while I do not carry the same cross that Hispanics do, I have known the blessedness of their struggle.

I see them as our best resource for a new Catholic counter-reformation, not a movement so much counter to Protestantism, but one that renews our own church. As the Holy Father has said, the new evangelization begins with the conversion of the evangelizer. The best way to attract and retain Hispanics or anyone else to the faith is for all of us to live it authentically, even counter-culturally. Hispanics may serve in the same way that visionaries do: as ordinary people with extraordinary faith who simply wish to share that faith through our pulpits and prelatures.

The resistance of mainstream Catholics will not mean that Hispanics will forfeit Christianity. The Protestant denominations that they join include millions of sincere Christians. Rather, resistance will mean the forfeiture of critical aspects of our own Catholic history and spirituality. My colleagues in this book recall in subsequent chapters the "original fervor" of the United States Catholic Church and how it remains a promise and a blessing.

PASTORAL CARE OF CATHOLIC SOUTH AMERICANS LIVING IN THE UNITED STATES

Fanny Tabares

Traditional patterns of immigration from Latin America to the United States resemble a series of concentric circles extending from the southern border of the United States into Mexico and the Caribbean. The phenomenon of globalization, which involves the compression of time and space, has resulted in increased interaction between people of the northern and southern hemispheres. Such globalization has created in more recent years a broadening of the immigration pattern to include an increasing number of South Americans. Commercial negotiations, such as the possible inclusion of Chile or other South American countries in a free trade agreement with Canada, Mexico, and the United States, will have significant implications for an integration of cultures and lifestyles.

Over the past twenty years much has been written about ministry among Hispanics or Latinos in the United States. Most literature, however, focuses on Mexican, Puerto Rican, and Cuban American communities, which are numerically the largest. However, with 26.5% of the worldwide Catholic population calling South America home, this continent will play an ever more important role in the life of the church in the United States. A careful analysis of this reality is timely.

South America: A Complex Reality

From the Amazon basin, which provides much of the world's oxygen, to the soaring Andes, second only in height to the mountains of Asia, to the coastal plain, the driest desert in the world, and to the gates of Antarctica, South America is a place of extremes.

By virtue of its Iberian heritage, a common language and history unite the South American continent. However, this continent of 6,880,638 square miles is incredibly diverse. Extending 1,000 miles north of the equator and 4,000 miles south, its population is as varied as its landmass. The 300 million people of the South American continent are of indigenous, African, European, Middle Eastern, and

9

Asian backgrounds. Geography and altitude have much to do with their characteristics. The traditions of many South American countries are markedly different when comparing the mountains to the jungles to the coast. Altitude and longitude are as culturally formative as national borders. Certain regions of South America are populated primarily by indigenous people, such as the highlands of Ecuador, Peru, and Bolivia. Countries comprising the Cono Sur, Chile, Argentina, Uruguay, and Brazil share a European immigrant experience not unlike that of the United States.

In the early 1900s, the population of South America was 70% rural and 30% urban. Rapid urbanization has taken place in most areas of Latin America, reversing these figures. Currently in South America, 70% of people live in cities and only 30% in rural settings. Large segments of the South American population have a highly developed political conscience. In some areas the military has exercised an important role in national politics.

Boundary disputes have periodically arisen between many South American nations (for instance, Ecuador with Peru, Bolivia with Chile, Colombia with Venezuela, and Argentina with Chile). Political, military, and national concerns often resurrect these disputes.

Some 80% to 90% of South Americans identify themselves as Catholic. The relationship between church and state varies from country to country. In Colombia, Peru, and Chile, for example, Catholic religion classes are mandatory in public schools, while in Argentina this is not true.

The economy of South America is closely tied to First World economic interests. The extraction of minerals is important in Chile (copper), Peru (silver), Bolivia (tin), and also in Venezuela, Colombia, and Ecuador (petroleum). Livestock and agriculture play important roles in Argentina (beef and grain) and in Brazil (citrus). Fish and seafood are important in Peru and Chile. Manufacturing is highly developed in Brazil, Argentina, and Chile. Textiles, coffee, and flowers are Colombian exports.

Another area that has affected the social, economic, and political reality of South America is narcotics. The climates of many South American countries lend themselves to the cultivation of plants used in narcotics production. For centuries coca was grown and utilized by local indigenous populations. An international network of drug traffickers now controls the cultivation, production, and distribution of narcotics world-wide. The enormous quantity of money generated through narcotic sales in First World countries, especially the United States, has purchased political favor, power, protection, and real estate for drug traffickers. This has resulted in much of South America experiencing increased violence, political and social instability, and a high cost of living, as well as ongoing involvement by the United States government in its internal political and military affairs.

Religious and Cultural Characteristics

South Americans enjoy not only a diverse cultural heritage, but also an integration of different religious expressions. The arrival of the Spaniards and the Africans in America resulted in the integration of three cultures into a spirituality with vivid religious expressions and symbols such as statues, celebrations of patron saints and feast days, and remembrances of the dead.

Many South Americans go to church only occasionally and for very concrete things such as ashes or palms or for the sacraments of baptism and first communion. However, if asked what faith they profess, they respond without hesitation, "Catholic."

There are specific programs for those groups and persons who wish to deepen their faith and have a more universal experience of church. However, in South America, and in general all of Latin America, much emphasis is placed on ministry to the masses. Ash Wednesday, Christmas, funerals, feast days in honor of the town's saints, Holy Week, alabados (especially on the coast and in towns of African influence), confessing one's sins before receiving communion (especially during Holy Week) are occasions of great celebration for numerous persons. Pastoral ministers are very conscious that these are formative moments when the faithful, especially men, are spiritually moved.

South Americans in the United States: The Demographic, Social, and Economic Situation

The 1990 United States Census recorded the following totals for Hispanics of South American ancestry: Colombia 351,000; Ecuador 197,374; Peru 161,866; Argentina 63,176; Chile 61,465; Venezuela 40,331; Bolivia 33,738; Uruguay 14,641; and Paraguay 5,415.

In 1960, Argentineans were the largest resident South American population in the United States, with Colombians second and Venezuelans third. Since then, a substantial influx of people from the Andean republics has made Colombia, Ecuador, and Peru the largest South American communities in the United States.

South Americans, when compared with other Hispanics, are dispersed throughout the United States. Excepting New York, no single state houses more than a quarter of the South American community. New York, California, Florida, and New Jersey are the states with the largest number of South Americans. New York has the largest number of Colombians and Ecuadorians. California is home to significant populations of Peruvians, Argentineans, and Chileans. Venezuelans favor Florida as a destination. For a variety of economic and governmental reasons, a disproportionate number of South Americans also reside in Washington, D.C. (Bean, Frank, and Tienda, Marta, *The Hispanic Population of The United States*. New York: Russel Sage Foundation, 1987, 101–102).

Among the five largest South American communities in the United States (Colombia, Ecuador, Peru, Argentina, and Chile), the percentage of foreign-born runs from 73% to 78% compared to only 33% of people of Mexican ancestry. Most South Americans living in the United States are recent immigrants.

The median age of South Americans living in the United States ranges from 30 to 34 years, depending on the country of origin. This compares to 24 and 25 years respectively for Mexicans and Puerto Ricans. The Cuban population is significantly older.

Educational attainment for persons of South American descent ranges from a high school completion rate of 61% for Ecuadorians to 82% for Bolivians. The rate for Mexicans is 44% and for Puerto Ricans 53%. Most South Americans come to the United States with a good basic education.

Among persons of Argentinean origin, 29% possess a bachelor's degree or higher, while 27% of Bolivians, 25% of Chileans, 16% of Colombians, and 12% of Ecuadorians do. In comparison, 9% of Puerto Ricans and 6% of the Mexican population have obtained the same degree. Many South Americans who immigrate to the United States are well-educated professionals. A large number of them are employed in managerial and professional positions, with an even larger number in technical, sales, and administrative work. Numerous Colombians and Ecuadorians are employed as machine operators, factory workers, and laborers. (See Table: U.S. Hispanic Population — March 1996 — Assembled by Institute for Puerto Rican Policy, pp. 19–20).

According to the 1990 census, median family income ranged from $30,000 for Colombians to $31,000 for Ecuadorians, $32,000 for Peruvians, $36,000 for Chileans, and $39,000 for Argentineans. This compares to $24,000 for Mexicans and $22,000 for Puerto Ricans. The income for Cubans is much higher than that of South Americans.

The proportion of South American families living at or below the poverty level range, from 8% to 15%, depending on country of origin. For Mexicans and Puerto Ricans, 23% to 30% of the families live at or below the poverty line.

Apparently many South Americans were part of the middle and upper classes in their homelands. Some came to the United States in search of economic and professional advancement, others for college or graduate studies. This usually ensures high self-esteem and an ability to situate oneself in a good job and adapt quickly to life in the United States.

Many Chileans and Argentineans come for political reasons. Beginning in the 1980s, immigration from Colombia, Bolivia, and Peru resulted from the economic and political crises these countries were facing. Drug trafficking and the violence this brings, not to mention economic sanctions imposed by the United States, are also important factors.

Many South Americans arrive in the United States with a resident visa obtained by the companies that employ them. Others arrive with a student or tourist visa. Still others cross the Mexican border without documents. Many are married to United States citizens. It is not uncommon to mortgage one's home or property to obtain the resources necessary to begin life in the United States, and to qualify for a tourist or student visa, which requires demonstrated economic solvency. Most South American immigrants do not come from settings of extreme poverty.

Several South American countries allow dual resident status. For example, Colombia does not require one to give up Colombian citizenship to become a United States citizen. For people of modest means, travel to South America is relatively infrequent due to distance and cost. Those of higher economic resources travel more frequently. Legal status in the United States facilitates one's coming and going.

For South Americans who reside in the United States without proper documentation, travel is more precarious. If they return home for a funeral, for example, their readmittance to the United States may be denied.

South Americans interact freely with the dominant Latino groups found in the United States. Common cultural, linguistic, social, and religious traditions promote this interaction. However, it is not uncommon for South Americans to feel out of place or unaccepted as a minority among the larger Hispanic community.

Stereotyping often creates isolation. Colombians, for example, are sensitive to outside perceptions regarding narcotics in their homeland, and often do not feel fully accepted by other Hispanics or Euro-Americans, (Gonzólez, Roberto, and La Velle, Michael, *The Hispanic Catholic in the United States: A Socio-cultural and Religious Profile.* New York: Northeast Catholic Pastoral Center for Hispanics, 1985, 158). (See: Comparative Statistics Table, pp. 21–22).

South Americans In The Church Of The United States

In general, Hispanics live a traditional, nostalgic, and conservative faith in order to preserve their identity and cultural roots and pass them on to their children. At times they are more conservative here than in their native country because they do not have as many possibilities to express and live their popular religiosity. Even though South Americans have been able to adapt to this country and settle in relatively well, the majority are still sentimentally attached to their country of origin and maintain communication with it by telephone, videos, and letters. Their experience at the core is that of a stranger in a strange land. For the most part, the church does not meet them in their exile. They have to integrate themselves the best they can into local parishes that generally are ill equipped to receive them.

Some parishes have tried to respond to the special characteristics of South Americans. We have, for example, celebrations of the Peruvian feasts of Senor de Los Milagros, Saint Martin de Porres, and Saint Rose of Lima; the Venezuelan feast of Our Lady of Coromoto; the Colombian feast of Our Lady of Chiquinquira; and the Argentinean feast of Our Lady of Lujan.

Priests and religious have rarely been able to immigrate here with their respective parishioners. However, many United States parishes and dioceses have contacted different Spanish-speaking countries blessed with vocations to ask for priests to serve the South American communities in the United States.

A significant number of South Americans find themselves in leadership positions within their parishes, dioceses, and on a national level within the church. With their Christian values of solidarity, hope, family unity, and almost a blind faith, they have responded admirably to the church here. With great sacrifice they have learned to accept as their own customs which, though Hispanic, originated in countries not their own.

The United States bishops see the Hispanic people as a prophetic voice and hope for the church. They encourage the faithful to defend life and to speak out for justice and solidarity. This posture of the church has helped many South Americans who have worked in base communities in their native countries. They follow a theology of liberation, and commit themselves to the poor, the immigrant, and the refugee. They strive to discover in history and in the present moment the call of God to develop a theology and spirituality from the perspective of the poor, the immigrant, and the Hispanic.

What can South Americans offer the church here in the United States? Their very presence calls the whole church to remember its universality, to work together for a church, indeed, a world where there are no barriers of race, culture, or language, but rather bridges uniting common hopes and dreams.

Pastoral Response

It is not easy to separate the gifts and the needs of South Americans from their culturally related Hispanic brothers and sisters. However, I will attempt to do so. Among the ministry proposals I would make are the following:

—Recognize and celebrate in the parish religious feasts special to different nationalities in such a way that no one feels excluded, and celebrate universal characteristics of different nationalities.

—Be conscious of the fact that many South Americans, though not yet able to communicate well in English, may be well prepared academically to understand the complexity of all that happens around them. They desire to continue forming themselves and deepening their integration into this society including the political, social, and religious aspects. They also have a deep thirst for God and wish to feel welcomed and recognized for who they are. They long to serve and to participate in their new church community.

—Generally, South Americans have high self-esteem and prefer to give rather than receive. For this reason, even though they have needs, they prefer to keep them to themselves rather than to ask for help. They feel humiliated being treated as the underprivileged poor. They are very proud of themselves, and the best way to relate to them is to ask for their help with some project or ministry.

—Many people from South America bring with them a highly developed social consciousness and can be of great help in parish programs that attend to social needs and welcome new persons in the community. Back home, many have put their lives at risk for others and have much experience of social and Christian commitment born of a serious study of a theology of liberation that reflects their experience of exodus and exile. The church must find ways to use to its best advantage this prophetic dimension.

—Statistics show that South Americans who come to this country are well prepared academically in ways that qualify them to serve as a bridge between the Hispanic community in general and the communities of other cultures, especially the European American. The parish should recognize and use this valuable gift in building up the whole church community.

—In general, South Americans come from cities where communication technology and life structures are more or less comparable to those of the United States. For this reason, it is easier for them to adapt to the world of technology in the United States than for those Hispanics who come from rural backgrounds. *Campesinos* who emigrate to the city from rural areas in their native lands find it difficult to adapt to an urban set of values and lifestyles. Their way of life, and how they relate to their families and to their neighbors, changes. People from South America can be of great service in helping others adjust to new urban environments.

—To be able to speak someone's language does not necessarily mean that one speaks from the same reality. It is important for people, particularly for South Americans, to understand the situation of those Hispanics who have come to this country not well educated, nor well adapted, nor with proper documentation. Some middle- and upper-class South Americans may not understand the discrimination and racism that some Hispanics have experienced in the United States because of their color or national origin. Parishes have a great responsibility to form their pastoral leaders so that their service in the community may be that of missionaries grounded in evangelical values. This involves sensitizing others, particularly middle- and upper-class South Americans and Latinos in general, to the plight of the disadvantaged.

—Parishes have to take into account that not all South Americans in the United States find themselves in privileged positions. Many South Americans suffer alone due to economic and social marginalization. As a minority group within the Hispanic community, and because of their reluctance in soliciting help, many suffer alone. By promoting social gatherings, parishes can gain a better understanding of the specific needs and gifts of individuals and groups within the Hispanic community and help them interact and come to know each other.

—Parishes at times put all Hispanics in the same mold, as if they all had the same education, same interests, and same life experience. Sometimes adult religious education for Hispanics has little content, fails to challenge, and is better suited for children. In these instances valuable leaders can be lost, including professional people who have skills in organizing and building community. The challenge is to develop adult-centered ministry which responds to different social and economic groups and to different pastoral needs, and to do ministry with a universal vision in which each person finds a place, feels welcome, and responds to the call to put one's gifts at the service of the church community.

— South Americans who have legal residence in the United States can be of great help to those who struggle in obtaining citizenship. They can speak in defense of the rights of immigrants and be a voice for those who cannot speak publicly for fear of being deported. The church, for its part, must make its voice heard more strongly in defending the rights of immigrants, taking to heart the gospel obligation: "I came as a stranger and you received me in your home" (Matthew 25:35). The church must be prophetic, announcing the good news of the kingdom of God today, and denouncing the ever-greater injustices and inequalities among different ethnic groups and even among white minorities. How can the United States church, in a world of consumerism and competition, make its preferential option for the poor? At times we think that the poor are only in other countries (*Economic Justice for All*, 170). But here in the United States many millions are poor, and many, by virtue of their undocumented status, find their rights severely limited. Only in walking together, sharing our gifts and our dreams, can we become the leaven of the kingdom of God in this young church of the United States.

—In general, South Americans speak Spanish at home and teach their children this language. They speak with pride to their children about their culture, their ancestors, their social and religious customs. This has helped young people feel proud of their ancestry, and though at times within social or educational settings they are singled out and made fun of, they are better equipped to feel secure in their identity. This high level of self-esteem nourished in the home provides a firm foundation for doing well professionally and academically in this country. Mastery of two languages has also contributed to their success on the university level. History teaches us that the way to destroy or diminish a culture from within is to forbid the use of its language and religion.

Conclusion

The church must offer a bilingual ministry, integrating children, youth, and adults in an open dialogue across generations, maintaining itself free of politics regarding language. Let us remember the words of Pope John Paul II when he came to the United States in 1996: "The Catholic Church also speaks Spanish." Hispanic youth ministry ought to proclaim the birth of a new culture. By recognizing the great potential of Hispanic youth as a symbol of hope and new life, the church of the United States will grow in number, quality, and Christian commitment.

This rich and marvelous new culture harmoniously incorporates various older ones. Like a symphony played by a variety of instruments, each appreciated for its unique sound, together they create a masterpiece. South Americans, in concert with others, have particular gifts and strengths needed to create this kind of church.

U.S. Hispanic Population - March 1996 - Assembled by Institute for Puerto Rican Policy

	Puerto Rican	Mexican	Cuban	Cent/South American	Other Latinos	Total Latinos	Non-Latino Whites	Total US Population
Estimated 1996 Population	3,123,000	18,039,000	1,127,000	4,060,000	2,089,000	28,438,000	191,271,000	264,314,000
Percent of Total U.S. Population	1.2	6.8	0.4	1.5	0.8	10.8	72.4	100.0
Percent of Latino Total	11.0	63.4	4.0	14.3	7.3	100.0	NA	NA
Median Age (years)	25.7	24.1	38.9	28.1	28.5	25.6	36.5	33.9
Percent Under 5 Years Old	10.3	13.3	5.0	10.1	9.7	11.9	6.5	7.6
Percent 18 Years and Older	61.7	61.4	81.1	68.7	68.2	63.8	75.9	73.1
Percent Female	53.8	48.3	48.7	50.8	50.4	49.4	51.0	51.1
Percent Married (15 yrs+)	45.8	56.3	56.8	52.3	49.2	54.0	60.2	57.0
Educational Attainment (% of those 25 yrs of age or older)								
Less Than 5th Grade	5.3	13.1	6.4	7.4	5.1	1C.3	0.6	1.8
H.S. Graduate or More	60.4	46.9	63.8	61.3	66.4	53.1	86.0	81.7
Bachelor's Degree or More	11.0	6.5	18.8	13.6	12.9	9.3	25.9	23.6
Labor Force Participation Rates (16 years of age or more) %								
Total	56.8	66.2	61.2	68.6	62.3	65.0	66.6	65.9
Males	66.5	79.8	69.4	79.4	72.9	77.4	74.1	73.9
Females	48.9	51.7	52.9	58.8	52.3	52.6	59.6	58.8
Unemployment Rates (16 years of age or more)								
Total	10.8	9.9	6.2	8.9	12.1	9.8	4.6	5.9
Males	10.1	9.6	6.5	7.8	16.0	9.7	5.1	6.6
Females	11.5	10.3	5.8	10.3	7.1	10.0	3.9	5.1
Selected Occupations (16 years & older) (% of workers)								
Males								

Managerial/Professional	15.6	9.6	21.3	10.4	22.0	11.6	30.5	27.3
Operators/Laborers	29.0	30.6	19.3	26.8	22.7	28.8	18.1	20.3
Females								
Managerial/Professional	22.7	16.1	22.9	14.5	19.1	17.2	33.1	30.5
Operators/Laborers	11.7	14.1	11.0	15.1	10.1	13.5	6.1	7.4
Median Earnings (1996)								
Females								
Part and Full-time	15,430	10,497	14,511	11,865	13,145	11,338	15,880	15,321
Percent of White Female Median	97.2	66.1	91.4	74.7	82.8	71.4	100.0	NA
Full-time Only	20,491	15,998	21,879	17,159	20,718	17,177	23,661	22,496
Percent of White Female Median	86.6	67.6	92.5	72.5	87.6	72.6	100.0	NA
Males								
Part and Full-time	20,018	14,717	21,445	15,978	18,028	15,653	27,252	25,017
Percent of White Male Median	73.5	54.0	78.7	58.6	66.2	57.4	100.0	NA
Full-time Only ($)	23,961	19,028	26,245	19,827	24,441	20,378	34,401	31,495
Percent of White Male Median	70.0	55.3	76.3	57.6	71.0	59.2	100.0	NA
Median Household Income (1995) ($)	19,605	22,552	25,186	25,994	23,282	22,860	37,378	34,076
Percent White HHD Average	52.5	60.3	67.4	69.5	62.3	61.2	100.0	NA
Total Persons in Poverty (1995)	1,183,000	5,608,000	108,000	246,000	50,000	8,574,000	16,267,000	36,425,000
Percent of Total Poor	3.3	15.4	0.3	0.7	0.1	23.5	44.7	100.0
Percent of Latino Poor	13.4	65.4	1.3	2.9	0.6	100.0	NA	NA
Poverty Rate for Persons (%)	38.1	31.2	21.8	24.8	25.6	30.3	8.5	13.8
% of Total Poor Under 18 Years Old	53.9	49.0	22.5	41.8	40.7	47.6	31.4	40.3

Feb. 16, 1998

3

20

Comparative Statistics Table

Characteristics for Persons of:	Colombian Number	%	Ecuadorian Number	%	Peruvian Number	%	Argentinean Number	%	Chilean Number	%	Puerto Rican Number	%	Mexican Number	%
All Persons	378,726		191,198		175,035		100,921		68,799		2,651,815		13,393,208	
Native Born	97,657	25.8	49,858	26.1	40,530	23.2	22,935	22.7	18,477	26.9	2,618,963	98.8	8,933,371	66.7
Foreign Born	281,069	74.2	141,339	73.9	134,505	76.8	77,986	77.3	50,322	73.1	32,852	1.2	4,459,837	33.3
Entered 1980-1990	145,567	51.8	61,749	43.7	83,195	61.9	30,889	39.6	21,202	42.1	15,494	47.2	2,247,960	50.4
Entered Before 1980	135,502	48.2	79,590	56.3	51,310	38.1	47,097	60.4	29,120	57.9	17,358	52.8	2,211,877	49.6
Naturalized	79,091	28.1	36,277	25.7	34,285	25.5	30,985	39.7	15,738	31.3	12,795	38.9	999,849	22.4
Not a Citizen	201,978	71.9	105,062	74.3	100,220	74.5	47,001	60.3	34,584	68.7	20,057	61.1	3,459,988	77.6
Median Age	30.4		30.1		30.7		34.4		32.3		25.5		23.8	
Education High School	67.1		61.1		78.5		75.5		78.0		53.4		44.2	
Bachelor and More	22.3		16.6		29.8		44.0		36.5		12.7		8.3	
Household Size														
3 Persons	21.4		19.8		19.9		19.3		20.9		20.7		17.5	
4 Persons	20.8		22.1		21.4		19.6		20.7		19.5		19.4	
5 or More Persons	21.4		28.0		23.8		13.6		17.3		20.7		33.7	
Speak a Language Other Than English	90.5		92.5		90.3		86.8		85.2		81.0		76.6	

Do Not Speak English "Very Well"	53.0		53.0		50.6		36.4		41.5		33.5		38.9	
Income in 1989 Family Median Income (dollars)	30,384		31,074		31,828		39,044		36,128		21,941		24,119	
Property Rate Families	13.1		14.6		11.7		7.8		8.2		29.6		23.4	
Occupation														
Employed Persons 16 Years and Over	195,240	100	98,957	100	94,445	100	57,951	100	36,949	100	925,893	100	5,323,210	100
Managerial and Professional	33,419	17.1	14,470	14.6	17,662	18.7	18,577	32.1	10,151	27.5	158,799	17.2	617,500	11.6
Technical, Sales, and Administrative	54,635	28.0	27,825	28.1	25,869	27.4	16,361	28.2	9,905	26.8	2,952,865	31.9	1,256,799	23.6
Service	42,207	21.6	18,749	18.9	22,399	23.7	8,682	15.0	7,038	19.0	170,934	18.5	987,215	18.5
Farming, Forestry, and Fishing	1,499	0.8	617	0.6	1,166	1.2	362	0.6	460	1.2	12,584	1.4	383,859	7.2
Production, Craft, and Repair	22,782	11.7	12,116	12.2	10,251	10.9	7,566	13.1	4,300	11.6	94,160	10.2	754,241	14.2
Operators, Fabricator, and Labors	40,698	20.8	25,180	25.4	17,098	18.1	6,403	11.0	5,095	13.8	194,130	21.0	1,323,596	24.9

(Source: United States Census 1990)

CHALLENGES TO THE PASTORAL CARE OF CENTRAL AMERICANS IN THE UNITED STATES

Kenneth G. Davis, O.F.M., Conv.

T his chapter deals with Central American populations. For each group it treats: 1) country of origin, 2) data specific to that particular people's situation in the United States, and 3) issues of pastoral care relevant to them. The conclusion presents broad ministerial recommendations and a suggestion for future collaborative research.

The term "Central America" commonly encompasses the five nations of Costa Rica, El Salvador, Honduras, Guatemala, and Nicaragua (some adding Belize and Panama). I will attend only to the last four countries. There are Costa Ricans in the United States, particularly in California. However, they are much less numerous than their fellow Central Americans.

The Winter 1998 *Hispanic Market Report* says that Central Americans in the United States number approximately 1.7 million. Forty-eight percent reside in the cities of Los Angeles, New York, Miami, and metro Washington, D.C. About 79% are foreign born. In general, people from this isthmus are older, more likely female, and slightly better educated than Mexican immigrants. They are even more highly urbanized. There is some friction between them and other persons of color, especially other immigrants (Wallace, Steven P., "Central Americans and Mexican Immigration Characteristics and Economic Incorporation in California," *International Migration Review*, Vol. 20 [1986], 657–671).

Hondurans

The second-largest but least populated of these countries, Honduras has historically been marginal even in Central America. After the mines played out, colonial Honduras was a backwater of the Spanish Empire. Consequently, there was little incentive for continued Iberian immigration. Therefore, the population is largely *mestizo* (mixed Spanish and Indian) with some few indigenous tribes

23

(*Hispanic Weekly Report*, Vol. 15 [3 February 1997], 3). Neither the efforts of the Mexican empire nor the United Provinces of Central America made the country more central to the region. Internal turmoil and external isolation continued until the early twentieth century.

By 1903 the Standard Fruit Company helped weld Honduras firmly into the neocolonial orbit of the United States. A series of military dictatorships brought a veneer of stability, but also presided over an economy that was (until the Sandinista revolution) the worst of all of continental Latin America. In the 1950s various labor unions won important victories; however, the so-called "Soccer War" with El Salvador in 1969 diverted popular attention (*Encyclopedia of Latin American History and Culture*. New York: Simon and Schuster, 1996).

Many attempted reform, but the military infiltrated or simply destroyed virtually all resistance. A persecution of the Catholic Church in the 1970s, particularly in Olancho, resulted in many murders, the loss of church institutions, the exile of a bishop, and a general chill on all reform attempts both within the church and without.

By 1984 Honduras had firmly established ties with the anti-Sandinista Reagan White House. Consequently, the military received considerable support. Increasingly this country was used as a base to resist the leftist groups in neighboring Nicaragua and El Salvador (*Latin American and Caribbean Contemporary Record*. New York: Holmes and Meier, 1985). Repression of labor movements and increased "disappearings" dispirited most organized opposition. As in El Salvador, the Jesuits were a notable exception to this reaction. Outside the north coast, mainline Protestant churches are still few. Of note are the Evangélicos' many social services; some organized to promote social justice by forming the Christian Development Commission (Barry, Tom, *Central America Inside Out: The Essential Guide to Its Societies, Politics, and Economics.* New York: Grove Weidenfield, 1991).

With the electoral defeat of the Sandinistas, and the peace accord in El Salvador, Honduras received much less military support in the 1990s. Moreover, various border settlements with its neighbors diminished the rationale for such a pervasive military presence. This has helped cause some strengthening of the civilian government relative to the military. However, years of corruption, dictatorship, and economic marginalization have left the country with little or no ability to compete in an increasingly technological world. Therefore, that same decade saw a boom in Honduran migration to the United States.

Hondurans may have come to this country as early as the 1830s; there is evidence of about 44 persons of Central American descent in that census. Their influx began to grow in the 1950s, and by the 1970s they were eliciting notice in New York and New Orleans. At first this was associated with the international fruit business. At that time they were the most numerous (31,000) Central American community in the United States, and the least racially white: Therefore, they drew attention. As with other Latino/a immigrants, they tended to gravitate to urban areas (*Harvard Encyclopedia of American Ethnic Groups*. Cambridge: Harvard University Press, 1980).

Los Angeles, New Orleans, and Chicago have significant Honduran communities. About 1,000 legally enter the country each year, and they are somewhat older than other documented Central Americans. There is evidence that wealthy Hondurans enjoy tourism in the United States. Of all Central Americans, Hondurans and Guatemalans received the fewest permits as refugees, presumably because their countries did not experience officially recognized civil strife (Reddy, M.A., ed. *Statistical Record of Hispanic Americans*. Detroit: Gale Research, Inc., 1995).

Over 200,000 Hondurans currently reside in the United States. Some estimate that almost 70,000 are here without legal documents. Immigration is still strong. Those who enter with the proper documents tend to be both socially and economically more stable (*Hispanic Link* [13 December 1993]; *The New York Times* [8 February 1997], A-7). Of the 131,066 Hondurans counted in the 1990 census, 77% were foreign born. Despite this, they made up only 1.5% of all foreign-born Spanish-speaking persons in the United States. Their median age was 27.5 years; about half have a high school diploma or equivalent. Unemployment was 12.2%, median household income $22,109. Over a quarter of Hondurans lived under the official poverty line. About one third worked in some white-collar occupation (*Hispanic Americans Today*, Washington, D.C.: Bureau of the Census, 1993).

As other Latino immigrants, Hondurans often migrate as clans. Entire villages in Honduras transplant themselves as extended families and settle in close geographic proximity within the United States. About 25% of them live in New York, 18% in Los Angeles, 14% in Miami, 7% in New Orleans, and 4% in Houston. Of all Latinos in

New Orleans, however, Hondurans make up 20%, therefore their higher profile there (Winsberg, Morton, "Specific Hispanics," *American Demographics* [February 1994], 44–53).

Like other Central Americans, Hondurans still do not generally have the long history or the dominant numbers to have organized much civic, church, or self-help associations. This was painfully evident after hurricane Mitch devastated the country. Relief efforts organized in the United States were initially stymied by this lack of organizational power. One exception is the Garífuna, an Afro-Carib minority within Honduras itself. This situation in their country of origin has forced them to value and maintain such close-knit social organizations even when emigrating (*Afro-Latin Americans Today: No Longer Invisible*. London: Minority Rights Publications, 1995).

Pastors face at least two pastoral care issues specific to Hondurans. First is racial discrimination. They are a largely mestizo population, and their darker skin can result in prejudice and discrimination. Second, Hondurans are perhaps the least likely Central American group to have a formal relationship to any church. The institutional Catholic Church in Honduras is so poor and weak (in a population of some 5 million there are only about 100 native priests) that it has never achieved great influence at any level of society. Hence, the number of unbaptized adults, and ignorance of Scripture, is remarkable. These issues need to be considered in pastoral care.

Salvadorans

They come from the smallest and most densely populated country of the isthmus. Although subordinated in colonial times to Guatemala, they trace the roots of their independence partly to the indigenous Nahuatl population. In 1856 they became the last of the Central American republics to become completely sovereign, although well into this century tensions with neighbors flared periodically into violence.

A single-crop economy (first indigo then coffee) developed an oligarchy of large land holders who ruthlessly wielded power, exemplified in the massacre of 1932. A relative liberalization of the military was reversed after the 1969 war with Honduras. Sandinista success only led to further fear and therefore reprisals by the military. Civil war erupted. The murder of the popular Archbishop Oscar Romero while celebrating mass underlined the vulnerability of absolutely everyone to the insane spiral of violence. Persecution was not limited to Roman Catholics. The Baptists, Episcopalians, and especially the Lutheran Church suffered (*Central America Inside and Out*).

Salvadorans come from a modern city state; they are quite urbanized even before reaching the United States. About 75,000 Salvadorans were killed during the war that uprooted one in four; huge numbers emigrated between 1971 and 1994, mostly to the United States. Los Angeles now has more Salvadorans than any other city outside San Salvador. They are also quite numerous in New York, Washington, D.C., San Francisco, and Houston. They are the largest Central American community in the United States (Recinos, Harold J., *Who Comes in the Name of the Lord: Jesus at the Margins*. Nashville: Abingdon Press, 1997).

The 1990 census counted over 565,000 Salvadorans; this may represent only 40% of all those actually in the country. Similarly, official statistics rate their median age at about 26, unemployment at 10.5%, and median household income as $23,729. About 34% have a high school equivalency, yet over 22% live in poverty.

As with Hondurans and others, these official statistics deal almost exclusively with those who are here with documents. If one factors in the undocumented Salvadorans, for instance, the median income probably drops closer to $10,000. There is evidence that Central Americans with documents, particularly Salvadorans, are more likely to be entrepreneurs. The undocumented seem to be very much younger, and more likely of rural origin (*Focus*, Vol. 18 [Fall/Winter 1996–97]).

Of all Central Americans, Salvadorans received the only treatment even approaching favored status. While only about 3% received asylum, the Temporary Protected Status (later Deferred Enforced Departure Decree) in 1990 and extended through 1995 gave them the right to work. (See the first volume of the United States Commission on Civil Rights report *Racial and Ethnic Tensions in American Communities: Poverty, Inequality, and Discrimination*. Washington, D.C.: 1993).

However, relatively few Central Americans benefited from the 1986 Immigration Reform and Control Act since so many arrived in the United States after 1982. The recession of the 1980s, the successful lawsuits brought against the Sanctuary Movement, and successive anti-immigrant legislation have made life increasingly difficult for Salvadoran immigrants (Smith, Christian. *Resisting Reagan: The United States Central American Peace Movement.* Chicago: University of Chicago Press, 1996).

Compared with other Latino/a immigrants, Salvadorans are fairly politicized. They are used to organizing themselves, and often expect and accept the churches to be involved in organized activities that confront injustice. However, this is not universal. It is precisely the deep political differences among Salvadorans which has tended to divide them, even disrupting extended family networks so often crucial to immigrant survival. Moreover, after the civil war, El Salvador became the Latin American country most ravaged by violent crime. Membership in adolescent gangs is growing. Dealing with these dicey issues is a pastoral challenge of particular note when working with this group (Ferris, Elizabeth G., ed., *The Central American Refugees.* New York: Praeger, 1987).

Guatemalans

This community comes from the most populous country in Central America, and the one with the most indigenous inhabitants, including Quichés, Chujes, Acatecs, and Kanjobales. Independence in the early nineteenth century led to a landed coffee elite by its end. Successive military dictatorships began to weaken in the 1930s but a 1954 military coup ended this reform. A return to civilian government in 1986 did not mean a return to peace. Not only was there an unsuccessful coup attempt in 1993, but human rights abuses, particularly against indigenous populations, continued. During this, the longest civil war in Central America, some 200,000 people perished and another one million fled their homes (Human Rights Office of the Guatemalan Church, "Guatemala: Never Again," 1998). Prospects for peace, however, increased dramatically with the efforts of Nobel Peace Prize winner Rigoberta Menchu (Burgos-Debrary, E., ed., *Rigoberta Menchu.* London: Verso, 1984).

March 1988 saw the Catholic Church begin a much more explicit campaign for social justice than in previous decades. However, the fastest growing congregations came from non-mainline Protestants. Not all of them mirrored the policies of Ríos Mont; Catholics joined with some to form the National Campaign for Life and Peace. In general, the public role of Christians in the political life of Guatemala has been historically important. However, the church's influence is still often minimal. A Catholic bishop was recently murdered soon after submitting a human rights report critical of the military.

Immigrants from Guatemala are perhaps the most rural, especially those settling in Florida (*The New York Times* [24 October 1991], A-18). In the 1980s their plight was particularly desperate, but a class action suit helped the rate of their asylum approval increase by more than sevenfold. Urban areas where they concentrate are Los Angeles, New York, Chicago, San Francisco, and Washington, D.C. However, even in Los Angeles they make up less than 1% of the total population.

Official statistics state that 80% of Guatemalans in the United States are foreign born, 38% completed high school, 10.2% are unemployed, and 21.1% live in poverty. Median household income is over $24,500, and the median age is 27 (*The Latino Encyclopedia*. New York: Marshall Cavendish, 1996). Those who work with Guatemalans suspect that, especially for the indigenous, these figures are quite optimistic (*The New York Times* [30 January 1997], A-1 and A-2). However, a 1998 report by Cara Anna of Cox News Service highlights their hopes of achieving greater legal protection from the United States government.

Persons ministering to Guatemalans in the United States must be particularly sensitive to the riches and special needs of the indigenous populations. Very few resources are available to pastors who wish to learn the language or scholars who simply wish to understand the situation. Perhaps groups such as the Asociación para la Educación Teológica Hispana, the Program for the Analysis of Religion Among Latinos, or the Academy of Catholic Hispanic Theologians of the United States can help to remedy this situation.

Nicaraguans

This is the largest of the Central American countries. That fact and their very high birth rate have not meant an enormous population. However, its geographic location, including the lake of Nicaragua, made it a victim of repeated invasions by British and United States soldiers of fortune who wanted to create a transoceanic canal during the nineteenth century. Formal United States government intervention began early the following century, its most infamous chapter being the occupation of the country in the 1930s, which included the repression of Augusto César Sandino and the installation of the Somoza dynasty.

Sandino died but his cause resurrected in the successful Sandinista insurrection of 1979. At first the Catholic Church and mainline Protestants generally supported the revolution. However, once the Sandinistas were firmly in power, this religious consensus deteriorated and was an important factor in the 1990 election of rival Violeta Chamorro.

Under the Sandinistas the country suffered tense and sometimes violent relations with the United States. The civil war and subsequent internal tensions, including battles with the contras, led to the emigration of up to 18% of the population (Umanzor Alvarado, R.A., "Las Migraciones Internacionales en Centroamerica en la Decada de los Noventa: Causas, Implicaciones y Consecuencias," *Estudios Migratorios Latinoamericanos*, Vol 23 [1993], 31–52). Even those who remained often hedged their bets by sending investments and some family members out of the country.

As refugees from communism, the first Nicaraguans arriving in the United States were fairly well received, at one point accounting for almost one third of all political asylum granted by our government. That favorable situation, however, is changing.

Nicaraguans are somewhat older than other Central American immigrants, and more urban. Greater Miami is home to over 150,000 Nicaraguans, making them the second largest Latino group in Dade County. Los Angeles, San Francisco, New York, and Washington, D.C. also contain large numbers (*The New York Times* [21 March 1995], A–1, A–12).

Sending economic support to loved ones back home preoccupies all Central American immigrants. However, Nicaragua's economy has suffered a steeper decline than any other in the last twenty years. Therefore that difficulty, coupled with the increasing complication in maintaining their legal status or arranging for the arrival of family members, is particularly acute within this population (*The Village Voice* [22 January 1991], 27, 41–42).

As with others, particularly Hondurans, hurricane Mitch will continue to influence this country and its compatriots in the United States. If the home economy does not recover, immigration to the United States will increase. The government of the United States is sending aid in a bid to stymie that new influx, and is attempting to help the home countries by slowing the deportation of Central Americans to their home countries now even less able to deal with returned (now unemployed) persons.

Ministerial Recommendations and a Research Suggestion

Pastors must first become intimately knowledgeable of their local community. This includes the ecclesial community he or she serves, the organizations that can or do serve Central Americans, and the greater community especially regarding its attitude toward these people in its midst. What follows are some general observations that may be helpful as a pastor intentionally observes and studies her or his community.

Central Americans share certain challenges common to other Latinos and Latinas. Among these are high rates of poverty, unemployment and underemployment, and associated low rates of decent housing, insurance, and access to banking services. While Central American immigrants appear on average to be relatively well educated, this does not necessarily translate into economic opportunities. Many foreign professionals are not accepted here and therefore labor at menial tasks. Crime, alcohol, drugs, poor public services, and high costs of living are associated with urban barrios. However, rural areas may not have even the minimal support services (especially in languages other than English) that cities offer.

Undocumented immigrants face other challenges. Roger Hernández estimated in 1997 that 50,000 Guatemalans, 60,000 Nicaraguans, and 190,000 Salvadorans could be deported. Lack of proper papers makes education and employment even more difficult and a willingness to cooperate with state institutions (e.g., hospitals, schools, police) more frightening. The need to provide for family in the home country exacerbates the immigrant's own precarious economic situation. Larry Rohter of the New York Times News Service estimated in 1997, for instance, that Salvadorans sent $1.25 billion home, representing 12% of that country's gross national product. Families are divided by borders, and immigrant families are divided by levels of acculturation. Children who have learned English and the intricacies of modern society sometimes take on the roles of parents. Families often spend much time apart, and this can lead to abrupt changes in family systems and/or the creation of more than one set of dependents.

Central Americans, however, find it even more difficult to maintain cultural contact or familial communications with their home countries because of the distances and international boundaries between the United States and that isthmus. Moreover, other nations dominate the Spanish-language media in this country.

There is at least anecdotal evidence that other Latinos and Latinas sometimes eye Central Americans with suspicion. Perceived competition for jobs, public funds, and political power creates tensions. Although non-Hispanics often refer to Central Americans as Mexicans, Puerto Ricans, or Cubans, they themselves know that they are doubly invisible. Anglos see them as another brown face, but the more dominant Latino communities may also maintain them on the margins (*Time* [13 June 1983], 18–25). And generally Central Americans do not yet have the history to have created their own strong social or ecclesial organizations (Ojito, Mirta, "Central Americans," *The New York Times* [25 March 1998], A-20). Internal disunity, and a common immigrant feeling that their stay in this country is temporary, complicate the situation (Cordova, Carlos. "The Social, Cultural, and Religious Realities of Central American Immigrants in the United States," in, A.M. Pineda and R. Screiter, eds., *Dialogue Rejoined: Theology and Ministry in the United States Hispanic Reality.* Collegeville: The Liturgical Press, 1995).

Perhaps the most important distinguishing pastoral concern is the incredible level of violence these people suffer. Many have been threatened, beaten, jailed, or tortured in their home countries (*The New York Times* [9 August 1996]). Some feel guilty for having survived (*Research Bulletin* [Spring 1987], 5–6).

Many have experienced warfare or seen loved ones die. Others live with the open wound of not knowing what happened to friends or family who simply disappeared. Hurried, secretive departures left no time to bring closure to relationships of a lifetime.

Perhaps even more have been victims of crime or official corruption before and during their journey North. We are just beginning to document the horrors both the Mexican and United States authorities have inflicted on these people (*El Visitante Dominical* [25 August 1996]). Depression, post-traumatic stress disorder, psychosomatic symptomatology, and domestic violence are often the result of this suffering (Dorrington, Claudia. "Central American Refugees in Los Angeles: Adjustment of Families and Children," in R.E.

Zambrana, ed. *Understanding Latino Families: Scholarship, Policy, and Practice*. Thousand Oaks: Sage Publications, 1995).

Again, it is obviously vital to understand the background of each congregant. Moreover, there is a substantial body of literature which shows that trained clergy can be particularly helpful to Latinos and Latinas who need counseling. However, many clergy do not have the training necessary to provide this level of counseling. Those who do, and who also have the requisite cultural and linguistic background, are few. And they may be unable, precisely by virtue of their licensing boards or institutional employers, to attend to an undocumented, poor, inadequately insured community.

As a final recommendation, especially for future research, I would like to return to an idea I broached in my first book *Primero Dios* (Susquehanna, PA: Susquehanna University Press, 1994). Based on studies of two self-help groups, I have concluded that there are striking parallels between the dynamics of these groups and the *mutualismo* (mutual aid) which often exists among Hispanic extended families, fictive kin, community associations, etc. Further research has led me to be even more convinced of the great potential pastors have in linking their communities with self-help organizations (*Apuntes*, Vol. 12 [Fall 1992], 127–136). I hope to continue this research, and I invite the collaboration of other interested scholars and pastors. We need a sustained, ecumenical, and interdisciplinary approach; I urge it upon all persons of goodwill.

DOMINICAN IMMIGRANTS: SOCIAL AND RELIGIOUS CONTEXT

Anneris Goris

The most interesting facet of the Latino migration to New York is its intra-Latino diversity. Dominican immigrants are estimated as the second largest Latino immigrant group in the city. The percentage of immigrants from Central and South America and from Mexico is also on the rise. New York's Latinos are of different class status, income and educational levels. Many speak Spanish, some only English, and others code-switch languages depending on circumstances. This population also represents different religions, races, and nation-states. The majority is Catholic, but there are Protestants, Espiritistas, and Santeros, (Stevens-Arroyo, Anthony M. and Andrés I. Pérez y Mena, Eds. NYC: Bildner Center for Western Hemisphere Studies, 1995. *Enigmatic Powers: Syncretism with African and Indigenous. People's Religions Among Latinos*).

Dominican Exodus to the United States

Large numbers of Dominicans have relocated to the Upper West Side of Manhattan. Colombians inhabit Queens and Puerto Ricans are in Manhattan, Brooklyn, and the Bronx. To understand the process of community development among Dominicans, emigration flow to the United States needs political, social, and religious context. This chapter attempts to do that.

Along with Puerto Ricans and Cubans, Dominicans started to emigrate to the United States at the turn of the century. The ships that brought Puerto Ricans and Cubans to the United States in the 1910s and 1920s also transported Dominicans to Ellis Island. (Anneris Goris, *The Role of the Ethnic Community and the Workplace*. Fordham University, 1994). In the late 1910s, Dominican women emigrated to the United States in search of work. Like Puerto Ricans, some of these women became machine operators in the garment industry. Dominican men worked in the manufacturing and service sectors. Small emigration streams of the previous decade continued and Dominican immigrants relocated in Manhattan and the Bronx. By the early 1930s, there were small pockets of Dominicans in the city, probably fewer than 1,000. However, both the Great Depression Dominican governmental policies reduced the attractiveness of emigration to the United States.

What helped to create the mass Dominican migration in the second half of the 20th century were structural and political changes in that island republic. The United States invasion of the Dominican Republic in 1916, and its occupation until 1924, left a well-established economic, military, and political apparatus in power.

In the Dominican Republic, Rafael Leonidas Trujillo Molina dominated the political and economic life of the nation, controlled the armed forces and elections, and eventually assumed the presidency for 30 years (1930–1961). From the early 1940s to the late 1950s, Trujillo, who feared that Dominican exiles would organize opposition political movements, controlled emigration from the island. During this period, emigration occurred on a very small scale and many of the visas were temporary. People desiring to leave the country were subjected to investigations (despuraciones) that included several interviews and official searches. If the government cleared the potential immigrants, they then were asked to pay a high fee for the passport book (over $300). Dominicans in the United States were required to register with the Dominican Consulate. Dominicans residing in this country were also fichados (tagged) by Trujillo.

Before 1960, there were about 5,000 Dominicans in the United States. Many were considered political exiles. Until the mid-1960s, emigration was not a realistic "escape valve" for the mass of Dominicans. After the assassination of Trujillo in 1961, the country underwent drastic social, political, and economic reorganization. Dominican workers detached from the agricultural labor force were able to offer their labor to local sectors of a cash economy. This process triggered a "redundance" of workers that in turn led to a reduction in labor price and a "surplus population." These "floating workers" became potential Dominican emigrants (labor) destined for exportation primarily to the United States (Goris, A. *Dominican Immigrants in the United States*. New York City: The Dominican Research Center, 1990).

In 1965 the Dominican Republic experienced a Civil War which was abruptly ended by the invasion of Unites States troops. The end of the overt strife coincided with a change in United States immigration law. This radically increased the number of immigrants allowed into the United States from the Western Hemisphere. Some Dominicans who emigrated during this period are referred to as Dominican hot heads (cabezas calientes). These were men and women who resisted the 1965 invasion and had little recourse but to flee the Dominican Republic because they feared reprisal from the regime installed with United States assistance.

That political crisis marked a new era in United States/Dominican relations: Dominican nationals would be exported to the United States as cheap labor, and United States multi-national corporations would be relocated to the island in search of raw materials and markets. In the mid-1960s the United States—imposed Balaguer regime facilitated the incorporation of the Dominican labor participation and capital flow into the international economy. The establishment there of free trade zones in the late 1960s resembles the economic development plan implemented in Puerto Rico by the United States twenty years earlier. The Dominican Republic was transformed from sugar production into a population exporting country and a target for the transnationalization of United States capital. It was swept into the process of economic restructuring and the globalization of production (Sassen, Saskia, *The Global City: New York, London, Tokyo*. New Jersey: Princeton University Press, 1991).

Massive emigration from the Dominican Republic to the United States coincided with the return migration of thousands of Puerto Ricans between 1965 and 1970. The low-paying jobs Puerto Ricans refused to accept, Dominicans would gladly take. Puerto Ricans who remained in New York City were likely to view the newcomers as competitors for jobs and resources and were pitted against them. The resurgence of Puerto Rican migration to the United States in the mid-1970s, though now not necessarily directed to New York City, also coincided with continuous emigration from the Dominican Republic to the Big Apple.

For over 30 years the Dominican Republic has experienced considerable population outflow to the United States. However, the exact size of the Dominican immigration population in the receiving nation is yet unknown. Larson, M. and Sullivan, T. (*Conventional Numbers in Immigration Research: The Case of the Missing Dominicans*. Texas Population Research Center Paper no. 9.010, 1987) estimate that over 500,000 Dominicans resided in the United States in the late 1980s. Other sources have placed the count at 903,650 between 1966 and

1984. Between 1981 and 1990, 251,803 Dominicans emigrated to the United States and 30,000 entered Puerto Rico, another bridge for this migratory flow. P.M. Graham ("Defining the District and Re-imagining the Nation: Transnational Political Practices Among Dominican Migrants," Ph.D. Dissertation, University of North Carolina, Chapel Hill, 1996) states, however, that during the period 1955–1990, a total of 3,078,831 non-immigrants were admitted from the Dominican Republic (people allowed to enter with temporary visas). A total of 679,199 entered as immigrants with permanent residence during this period.

Today, Dominicans comprise the third largest source of immigration to the United States from Latin America with an emigrant population estimated at over one million documented, undocumented, and the children of Dominican nationals born in the United States (Mann, E., and Salvo, J., "Characteristics of New Hispanic Immigrants to New York City: A Comparison of Puerto Rican and Non-Puerto Rican Hispanics." Paper presented at the Annual Meeting of the Population Association of America, Minneapolis, MN. May, 1984).

With a relatively small Island population of around eight million (about the official population of New York), these one million Dominicans in the Unites States represent a sizable percentage (12.5%) of the republic's total population. Perhaps more Dominicans live in New York than those inhabiting Santiago de los Caballeros, the second largest city in the country founded by Columbus in 1500.

Community Development Among Dominican Immigrants

Like other immigrant groups, Dominicans have also constructed their own ethnic community in the United States. A large number of Dominicans reside in Washington Heights/Inwood, in northern Manhattan. The clustering of the Dominicans in this neighborhood has inspired some to call the area "Quisqueya" or "Dominican Heights."

Washington Heights/Inwood was built after the turn of the century as a residential area for second- and third-generation Irish Catholics and Jewish immigrants who sought refuge from slums farther south. This working-class part-time community was "spatially separated from where most of its residents worked." The neighborhood was close to a "typical capitalist residence community," and "ethnic dimensions of community life helped to cohere a class society, even in the midst of the Great Depression." The community was a "pristine example of the separation of work and home, and of classes from each other" (Katznelson, I. *City Trenches: Urban Politics and the Patterning of Class in the United States.* New York: Pantheon Books, 1982).

In the past, this type of community tended to shape the residents' entire identity. For some people, "the neighborhood provided the most tangible experiences and ties of daily life" (Mann and Salvo). More recently, however, the networks of the main groups (Jews, Irish, Blacks, Cubans, and Dominicans) define the contours of relationships and the daily experience of residents inside and outside the community. Dominicans may confine their system of networks to compatriots and other Latinos who reside there such as Cubans, Puerto Ricans, and more recently, Mexicans, Central and South Americans. Outside the area, Dominicans have also built coalitions with other Latino groups.

Dominicans, however, are not the dominant ethnic group in the area. But they represent the largest Latino group with a rapidly growing demographic potential. The music played on the street is Dominican merengue, old-time Dominican songs, and música de campo a dentro, de guardia y de barra (peasant or country, military, and bar music). Over 80 percent of the bodegas (small groceries) in New York City today are owned and operated by Dominicans. Thus, in Washington Heights/Inwood, a Dominican entrepreneur class caters to the needs of the community by providing all kinds of merchandise from the homeland. Dominican ethnic foods and restaurants are scattered throughout.

There is a flourishing cultural movement comprised of many groups that promote Dominican poetry, theater, arts, and dance. The Dominican Day Parade celebrated in August brings every form of Dominican cultural expressions to a citywide audience. Many Dominican associations have headquarters in the area. Daily newspapers from the Dominican Republic are sold in almost all the newsstands. And the numbers of Dominican businesses are increasing. Also, according to statistics from school district #6 and the Education Office of the Archdiocese of New York, over 80 percent of the students in both public and Catholic schools are Dominicans.

Over the years, Dominican immigrants have formed numerous community-based organizations, associations, and clubs to deal with different issues and problems (Georges, E., *New Immigrants and the Political Process: Dominicans in New York.* New York: Center for

Latin American and Caribbean Studies, New York University Research Program in Inter-American Affairs. Occasional Papers 45, 1984). It is estimated that more than 100 of these institutions are located in Washington Heights/Inwood (Jenkins, S., Sauber, M., and Friedlanders, *Ethnic Associations and Services to New Immigrants in New York City.* New York: Community Council of Greater New York, 1985).

In the season ending in September 1998, Sammy Sosa, a Dominican baseball player with the Chicago Cubs, batted 66 home runs, breaking the Latino record. He was welcomed to New York City in October with a citywide celebration organized by Mayor Rudolph Giuliani. The Dominican community, however, fought to have Sammy visit Washington Heights. After the downtown appearance, he went uptown to be with his Dominican fans. Sammy finished a very emotional speech affirming his cultural and national identity: Soy Dominicano, eso es lo que soy (I am Dominican and that's what I am) and danced merengue to further reinforce his sense of Dominicanness. The Catholic Church also honored Sammy in a mass at Saint Patrick's Cathedral offered for victims of Hurricane George that killed hundreds of people in the Dominican Republic.

Community-based organizations have provided direct services to Dominicans in New York City. Studies on the development of organizations among Dominicans found that they form "affective" associations. S. Sassen-Koob ("Formal and Informal Associations," *International Migration Review* [Summer, 1979]) states that the organizations are "rooted in the nature of the gap between place of origin and receiving society." Dominicans form social and recreational voluntary associations in New York City, in part due to their rural background and class origin on the island.

In a later study in which Dominican community leaders were interviewed, Georges proposed that the proliferation of voluntary organizations among Dominicans was indicative of the adjustment process that the group was experiencing rather than a lack of integration into the receiving society. Georges found that members of the associations constitute a highly exclusive group of well-educated people who come to New York City at an early age. Participation rates in neighborhood associations by women are lower than those for men, but females are very likely to belong to church organizations.

Jenkins, Sauber, and Friedlanders found that Dominican associations changed their initial purpose over time, as did community-based institutions developed by earlier immigrants. This study also underscores the important role that Dominican organizations play in helping the group obtain necessary social services. For example, Asociaciones Dominicana provides services to children, youth, and adult classes. Alianza Dominicana operated in the 1990s with a budget of over $4 million. It has begun to diversify its services to include youth programs, AIDS workshops, and cultural events. El Centro de la Mujer Dominicana has literacy classes in Spanish, English, and workshops on Dominican women's issues and computer training classes.

Coalitions between Dominicans and Puerto Ricans have also facilitated the inclusion of Dominicans in the political system. For example, in the early 1980s State Assemblyman Jose Rivera and State Senator Olga Mendez pressured Governor Cuomo to assign a Dominican representative to the statewide Committee for Hispanic Affairs. In 1983, Eduardo Cuesta, a Dominican community activist, became part of that committee. Senator Mendez also suggested that Julio Hernandez be elected as a district leader with her help. Interethnic group cooperation between Puerto Ricans and Dominicans in Washington Heights has facilitated access to organizational resources. These alliances have helped Dominicans gain inside knowledge about how the local political machinery functions. Dominicans seem to be following similar types of community organizing strategies used by Puerto Ricans to develop a community-based power structure.

Religion: A Survival Mechanism for Dominican Immigrants

Irish immigrants of the nineteenth century were able to transplant their Catholic Church to the "new land." Clergy came with them. The church was, therefore, the first, most important and most significant institution that the Irish immigrants established. It provided a sense of identity and became the center of life in the immigrant community. M. Smith ("Networks and Migration Resettlement: Cherchez La Femme," *Anthropological Quarterly* [49, Vol. 1], 1976) points out that for all such immigrants the church was the place where they felt the security and the identity which flow from a structured system of values and relationships. Robert Bellah (*The Broken Covenant: American Civil Religion in a Time of Trial*. New York: The Seaberg Press, 1975) asserts that it also provided an essential link between the ethnic group and the larger society. The Catholic Church was also instrumental in the incorporation process of Italians in the United States. The national parish was an important instrument created by early immigrants to preserve their culture, customs, language, and religion. In these parishes the immigrants felt a strong sense of community, native clergy ministered, and a semi-democratic process prevailed.

Latinos in the United States have had a different encounter with the church. Puerto Rican experience differed from that of earlier European Catholic groups in New York City (Fitzpatrick, J., *Puerto Rican Americans*. Prentice-Hall: Englewood Cliffs, NJ, 1987). They were received into an integrated church often staffed by non-Latino Spanish-speaking priests fostering assimilation into the already established Irish, Italian, or Polish parish. Masses and services were provided in Spanish, but often in a cold basement or a hallway. The integrated parish did not function as the basis of an immigrant or ethnic community for Latinos because the support commonly rendered in the national parish was not provided.

Dominicans, however, found a Catholic Church in New York City that had been sensitized to the needs of the Spanish speakers by decades of pastoral outreach directed toward the earlier mass migration of Puerto Ricans. Unlike the Puerto Ricans, they did not have to fight battles to have mass celebrated in Spanish, to organize parish agencies and church-based associations for their brand of Catholicism or struggle to gain recognition as a group different from earlier immigrants.

The Dominican struggle was a new one, an intra-Latino struggle. The secular tensions and competition with Puerto Ricans were often carried over into the parish. Nonetheless, while not minimizing the conflicts, on the whole Dominicans and Puerto Ricans were able to use the church as a space to construct a positive trans-Latino identity while not losing the specificity of their Dominican roots. By instituting special celebrations in the early 1970s, the unique character of Dominican Catholicism was confirmed. The mass for Nuestra Señora de la Altagracia, patroness of the Dominican Republic, was celebrated at Saint Patrick's Cathedral for the first time in the mid-1970s. Dominican clergy from the homeland were invited to participate. Jose Gutierrez, a member of JAC (Juventud en Acción Cristiana or the Christian Youth in Action Group) from Our Lady of

Sorrows Church, was the main organizer for this event (Goris, A. "Rites for a Rising Nationalism: Religious Meaning and Dominican Community Identity in New York City," in A. Stevens-Arroyo, and G. Cadena, Eds., *Old Masks, New Faces: Religion and Latino Identities*. New York, NY: Bildner Center, 1995). Misas cantadas (sung masses) and the enactment of biblical passages in which key events were staged inside the main chapel of the church also became important elements of the religious celebration.

But Dominicans joined with Puerto Ricans at worship in the Cursillos, Charismatic Movement, religious retreats, the diaconate, and in the pastoral commitments and social activism sponsored in different city parishes. The JAC provided a sense of continuity and community for Dominicans who made Our Lady of Sorrows their home away from home.

A study conducted in 1987 (Goris, A. "The Role of the Ethnic Community and the Workplace in the Integration of New Immigrants: A Case Study of Dominicans in New York City," Ph.D. Dissertation, Fordham University, 1994) shed light on the question of religious practices among Dominicans in Washington Heights and Inwood. Dominicans are overwhelmingly Catholic (86%). Only 7 percent were Protestants and the rest claimed to have no religion. More women (92%) than men (72%) reported their religious affiliation as Catholic. Sunday church attendance was 76 percent, with women attending more (75%) than men (70%). Nineteen percent go to mass during the holidays. These data confirm George's research indicating that immigrant women participate more often in church than immigrant men.

Research on assimilation suggests that length of residence has an important bearing on integration. To determine whether length of residence affects Sunday mass attendance, data among recent arrivals and longer-residing immigrants were compared (Goris, 1994). The data show that Sunday church attendance is low among Dominicans residing in the United States between 0 and 3 years (15%). But the rate seems to be higher among men (20%) than among women (18%). The group living in the country between 4 and 9 years also showed low participation (19%), but men are less likely to attend Sunday mass (7% compared with 16% for women). Those in the country for more than 10 years have the highest attendance (66%), with more men (73%) attending than women (67%). Longer-residing immigrants were more likely to have attended Sunday mass than recently arrived immigrants (see Table 1).

Table 1
Percentage Distribution on Selected Measures of Assimilation for
Dominican Immigrants in Washington Heights/Inwood, 1987

	Total	Women	Men
Religion			
% Catholic	86.2	91.9	72.1
% Catholics Attending Sunday Mass	76.0	75.0	69.8
% Catholics Attending Sunday Mass			
0–3 Years	15.0	17.8	20.0
4–9 Years	19.2	15.6	6.7
10+ Years	65.8	66.7	73.3
Total Number	167	123	43
Number Catholics	144	113	31

The distribution of the measures of religious participation by work-place location revealed interesting findings. The main concern was whether there were differences in church attendance among immigrants working in and outside of the community. The table shows that 98 percent of respondents working outside of the community are Catholic. More Catholics, therefore, are likely to work outside the ethnic community. Catholics working in or near the ethnic community are more likely to attended Sunday mass (89% compared with 77%). However, this difference is based on a small subsample size and may not be significant (see Table 2).

Table 2
Percentage Distribution on Selected Measures of
Assimilation by Location of Workplace:
Dominican Immigrants in Washington Heights/Inwood, 1987

	Far	In/Near
Religion		
% Catholic	97.7	86.3
% Catholics Attending Sunday Mass	76.7	89.1
Number Sample	44	117

An examination of those who attend Sunday mass by workplace and length of residence indicates that those Dominicans who have been in the country for less than 10 years and work far from the community attend Sunday mass more often than any other group. The rate of Sunday mass attendance was also moderate among Dominicans working outside the ethnic community and residing in the country between 10 and 20 years.

Based on these findings, we must ask: What do these data say about integration? To the extent that the church is a quasi-national parish, frequent attendance at mass would be expected of an immigrant community. However, at this point we must make two qualifications. First, in Latin America, church attendance is not necessarily an indication of religiosity. Second, Fitzpatrick's "integrated church" may not provide a strong sense of identity for the newcomers. However, a number of churches such as Incarnation, Saint Rose of Lima, and Saint Elizabeth located in the Dominican neighborhood may have become the equivalent of national parishes for the Dominican population in that zone. Looked at from American norms (frequency of mass attendance) this would suggest that length of residence and workplace impact church attendance.

Church attendance among Dominican immigrants in general is moderately high since mass attendance is in decline not only in the United States, but worldwide. Studies in the United States show that this has been the case since the 1960s. Andrew Greeley clarifies, however, that other forms of religious practices among Catholics are on the rise (*The American Church: A Social Portrait*. New York: Basic Books, Inc., 1977). For example, more people are attending charismatic prayer meetings, going to religious group discussions, performing informal liturgy at home, and receiving weekly communion.

In the case of Dominican immigrants, however, religious practice must be understood within the context of the Catholic faith in Latin America. There Catholicism is experienced more as a "community manifestation" and not as an individualistic or private affair. In Latin America, religion is a way of life. Latin Americans do not necessarily feel as compelled as Catholic Americans to be members of an organized church. For the former group religion provides, in the words of the late Father Joseph Fitzpatrick, "a sense of identity." It is for this reason that they perceive the church as a community to which they belong whether they attend church or not. Low church attendance does not necessarily imply a loss of religious faith among United States immigrants (Stevens-Arroyo, A., and Diaz-Stevens, A. *An Enduring Flame: Studies of Latino Popular Religiosity.* New York City: Bildner Center, 1994).

The present rates of church attendance among Dominicans in New York City may reflect an adaptation to forms of general United States religious practice. At certain times a church may undertake a special project or celebrate a public event to better appeal to a particular ethnic group. One such effort was centered on the execution of a Dominican held in a United States jail: unfortunately, the church that provided this outreach was not Catholic (Goris, 1995). It would appear that "Americanizing" Dominicans will take them away from the church. Clearly, new forms of pastoral care are necessary to combine ethnic and Catholic identities.

Marriage and Intermarriage Among Dominicans

The study on Dominicans in Washington Heights/Inwood conducted in 1987 found that in general more than half of the population sample was married (56%). Twenty-one percent of the participants reported their marital status as single; over 11 percent were divorced; 10 percent separated; and 2 percent were widowed. Most Dominicans have married other Dominicans. An examination of intra-Latino group intermarriage rates shows that a small but growing group married Puerto Ricans. Nearly 2 percent have Cuban spouses; and another 2 percent are married to either Panamanians or Ecuadorians. Out-group marriage was less than 10 percent. Research conducted by Fitzpatrick and Gurak of Latino marriage patterns in New York City found that 63 percent married with other Dominicans, 30 percent with other "Hispanics," and 8 percent with "other." Among Dominican grooms, 62 percent married Dominican brides, 32 percent other "Hispanics," and 6 percent with "other." Our findings of marriage rates among Dominicans, although lower in 1987, reflect the pattern described by Fitzpatrick and Gurak (*Hispanic Intermarriage in New York City: 1975, 1979*) 8 years earlier.

In general, they found high rates of intermarriage among second-generation Cubans, Mexicans, Central and South Americans with non-Latinos. Also, there was substantial intermarriage among the different Latino immigrants. Latina brides are more likely to experience out-marriage than Latino grooms. Intermarriage is usually higher for second-generation Latinos than for the immigrants. Rates of intermarriage among Dominicans and Puerto Ricans increased from 5 percent in 1975 to 19 percent in 1991. The rate of Puerto Rican brides marrying Dominican grooms increased from 6 percent to 21 percent during this period. First-generation Dominican grooms and Mexican brides had the lowest rates of intermarriage, while Cubans had the highest.

If intermarriage with individuals from the dominant social group is considered a strong indication of assimilation into the host nation, we can conclude that Dominican immigrants are not entering mainstream society by this route.

Marriages between Dominicans and Puerto Ricans in New York City are attributed to different factors. Gilbertson, Fitzpatrick, and Yang conclude that proximity, racial and cultural variables are important in explaining the high intermarriage rates between these two groups. In terms of race, Massey and Denton ("Residential Segregation of Mexicans, Puerto Ricans and Cubans in Selected United States Metropolitan Areas," *Social Science Research* 73 [1989], 73–83) found that there is segregation between black and white Latinos in the United States. However, Gilbertson, Fitzpatrick, and Yang ("Hispanic Intermarriage in New York City: New Evidence from 1991," *International Migration Review* XXX [2], 1996) conclude that since racial similarities are shared between Puerto Ricans and Dominicans, it is understandable that the intermarriage rates will also be high between them.

Concluding Remarks

I have tried to articulate different dimensions of the Dominican experience in the United States. I used a survey conducted in 1987 to integrate information gathered at the community level. The distributions on the variables of integration for the total sample and for men and women were viewed separately. To examine the hypothesis that immigrants working outside the community are more integrated into mainstream American society, findings from the comparison of immigrants working inside and outside of the community were presented earlier on this work. Little differences between the two groups of immigrants were found. The findings are summarized as follows: 1. Participation in the Church frames the experience of a large portion of the sampled Dominicans: 2. The majority of respondents identify themselves as Catholics and report that they attend Sunday mass: 3. Women were more likely to attend Sunday mass than men. 4. Longer-residing immigrants were more likely to attend Sunday mass than recent arrivals.

Much research suggests that length of residence has an important bearing on integration or assimilation (Gordon, 1964). To determine whether length of residence affects mass attendance among immigrants, we compared Sunday mass attendance among recent arrivals and longer-residing immigrants. The results presented in Table 1 indicate that longer-residing immigrants were more likely to have attended Sunday mass than recently arrived immigrants. The significance of these findings is discussed below.

The distribution of the measures of religious participation by workplace location revealed interesting findings. The main concern was whether there were differences in church attendance among immigrants working in and outside of the community. Results presented in Table 2 show that close to 90 percent of Catholic respondents working outside of the community attended mass compared with only 75 percent of Catholic respondents working in the community.

Given the above findings one must ask: What mechanism to integrate has the Catholic Church provided for Dominican immigrants in New York City and other Latinos in the United States? It has provided for the continuation of the faith without, however, the awareness that this type of gathering will enhance the maintenance of the "ethnic Dominican community" in exile. As stated above, religion in the homeland is a communal act, and it is not experienced, perceived, or viewed as separate from the community. When religion is a way of life, it permeates all aspects of the immigrants' daily existence. In a sense, the village concept of religious practice or of todo un pueblo en marcha (a whole people marching together) is difficult to reproduce in the receiving society. The alternative may be to settle for the continuation of the faith in exile.

Latino immigrants, therefore, do not need to re-create or re-make the institution in the diasporic experience. Rather they need to popularize the faith and to foster a different religious and cultural environment. For Latino Catholics, the worshipping place is not limited to the one constructed in the chapel or church. Home altars are created anywhere in the house. The concept that Dios (God) is everywhere often requires very little contact between the house of prayer constructed by the established church or determined by the priest and those made by el pueblo caminante de Dios (the people walking with God).

The colonial Catholic Church was Spanish in Latin America and the Caribbean. The integrated church that Fitzpatrick talked about was the institutional response of the Catholic Church to the religious and social adjustment needed by European immigrants in what was and continues to be a multi-religious nation. Those national parishes became the new form of American Catholicism. In essence, this type of church prevented a rupture between the different linguistic and ethnic groups entering the United States church. During this period "the diversity of the Church [was maintained] in such a way that the unity of the Church on the diocesan level was never threatened" because it was placed under "the jurisdiction of the bishop" (Fitzpatrick, J., *One Church, Many Cultures*. Kansas City, MO: Sheed and Ward, 1987). In the new world the Catholic Church also acquired characteristics of a middle-class institution. This was the type of Catholic Church—culturally pluralistic and upper class in structure —found in the United States by immigrants arriving later from the Caribbean, Mexico, Central and South America.

Today, as Latinos become the largest group within the church, United States Catholicism may need to adapt itself once more to different culture and class backgrounds. A crisis in the process of "inculturation," to use Fitzpatrick's term, would likely lead to a crisis in faith. The Catholic Church may stand to lose Latinos to other religions (Protestant) or to other practices such as Santeria, Espiritismo, or gaga. Hopefully, Latino Catholics have sought a balance between a pan-Hispanic tradition and the expression of nationalistic particularities. Dominicans present a challenge to that effort. Moving beyond stereotypes that presume that all Latinos are either Mexicans, Puerto Ricans, or Cubans, Dominicans demonstrate that the "other" Latinos have a force and a future. Dominicans too contribute to the continuation of the faith of the transplanted and exiled United States Catholic Church.

In the United States, redesigning the immigrant experience is more than just a quest for a new life. Religion and culture are two important variables reshaping the ethnic identity of newcomers. However, another integral part of this phenomenon, which should be explored by future research, is the metamorphosis from national group to the racialized "Other" experienced by many Latino/as. Subordination in terms of class and race means stripping groups of their language and culture. Both social memory and nationality are contested. For example, the classification of Dominicans as black in the United States (due to a high proportion of dark-skinned individuals within the group) has not gone unnoticed by that community. In actuality, the Dominican Republic is over 85 percent mulatto (mixed race). Racially, mulattos do not identify themselves as black, and constitutionally they are white or different shades of black. Officially, dark-skinned Dominicans are categorized as indios (Indians) and/or trigueños (wheat color). Moreover, the association of blackness with Haiti has reshaped part of the questions of national and ethnic identity. The entire island of Quisqueya (the indigenous name for Hispaniola) was more than once occupied by Haiti. This forms part of the collective memory of *el pueblo Dominicano* (the Dominican nation/people). For Dominicans, black is reminiscent of both their independence and also their Spanish ancestry. For Dominicans, the restructuring of the identity from indio to black is a political question as well as a racial and an ethnic transformation. Perhaps in the United States, hispanofilia is being replaced by a stronger sense of Dominicanness or national identity.

PASTORAL CARE OF *"LOS MARIELITOS"*

Adele J. González

Introduction

The last four decades of the second millennium will always be remembered in South Florida for the dramatic number of refugees and exiles that entered the area. Cubans, Nicaraguans, Haitians, and other Latin American and Caribbean groups arrived in the peninsula looking for political and religious freedom and economic opportunities.

One of the largest migrations took place shortly after Fidel Castro seized power in Cuba on January 1, 1959. More than 300,000 refugees crossed the 90 miles of sea that separate that Caribbean island and Key West, Florida. This early group was formed primarily by educated members of the middle classes. After several years of increasing tension between the and the United States (e.g., the failed Bay of Pigs invasion in April 1961 followed by the missile crisis of October 1962), a total rupture between those governments occurred during the Kennedy administration.

In 1965, after three years of separation from their families in the United States, Castro opened the seaport of Camarioca in the northern coast of Matanzas so that exiled Cubans could come back to pick up their relatives who wished to join them in the United States. This event was followed by the *vuelos de la libertad* (freedom flights) between Havana and Miami that lasted until 1971. During that period approximately 280,000 more Cubans arrived in Miami. This new group included workers, *campesinos* (farm workers), and members of the middle class. Many were the parents and relatives of Cuban children who had previously been sent alone to the United States in the early 1960s (Dolan, Jay, and Jaime Vidal, *Puerto Rican and Cuban Catholics in the United States, 1960-1965*, South Bend, IN: University of Notre Dame Press, 1994). The year 1965 also marked an increase in the number of people sailing the waters between Cuba and the Florida keys in small boats, rafts, inner tubes, and anything that would float. Many drowned trying to reach the United States.

Events Leading to the Mariel Exodus

In 1978, due to the unrest caused by the difficult living conditions on the island, that government allowed Cuban exiles to return and visit their relatives. Their intent had been to lure United States dollars into the economy. But they seriously underestimated the effect that these visits would have on the Cuban population. After two decades of isolation and anti-exile propaganda, the visitors became tangible proof of life in a capitalistic society that contrasted sharply with the island's poverty. As visiting relatives told stories about the abundant life in the North, protests and discontent became more frequent in Cuba. Children began to question their parents and the promises of the *revolución del pueblo* (the revolution of the people). According to statistics from the Cuban Refugee Program, there were more emigrants in 1979 (by boat, raft, etc.) than in all of the previous seven years combined (Clark, Juan, "Reflexiones en Torno a una Balsa," *The Miami Herald* [12 November 1979], 4). For a different view of this period, see Felix Roberto Masud-Piloto's *With Open Arms: Cuban Migration to the United States* (Totowa, NY: Rowan and Littlefield, 1988).

Meanwhile, mounting pressure from human rights groups and foreign governments forced Castro to allow former political prisoners to migrate to the United States. One of those who came during this period now lives in Miami with his family. His story is typical: Released in 1969 after nine years in a Cuban prison, he and his wife decided to leave the country via Spain. During the period of waiting, his wife, a school teacher, was not allowed to work; money became scarce and their living conditions deteriorated. After visiting the immigration office every week for ten years, they were finally granted permission to leave the island in February 1980. They told a story of frustration and unrest demonstrated for the first time in years with anti-government flyers and wall graffiti. It was during this volatile period that the events at the Peruvian embassy in Havana and the subsequent Mariel exodus began to unfold.

10,800 at the Peruvian Embassy

Sporadic attempts to enter Latin American embassies had happened before in Havana. But nothing compared with what took place in the afternoon of April 4, 1980. A few days earlier a Cuban guard had accidentally been shot while attempting to prevent a bus carrying some twenty Cubans from penetrating the Peruvian embassy compound. This incident prompted Castro to announce the removal of the entire Cuban military guard from that embassy. Within the twenty-four hours that the embassy lacked military protection, 10,800 Cubans from both outlying provinces and the Havana area entered the Peruvian compound (Clark, Juan M., Jose I. Lasaga, and Rose S. Reque, "The 1980 Mariel Exodus: An Assessment and Prospect," *A Special Report of the Council for Inter-American Security*. Washington, DC, 1981). These events attracted world attention and seriously threatened the image of a Cuba where everyone was content.

The Massive Mariel Exodus

To respond to the crisis, the Cuban government agreed to allow the thousands who had sought refuge at the Peruvian embassy to fly to a country willing to receive them. Costa Rica agreed. The sight of women, men, and children arriving in that Central American country looking for freedom tarnished Castro's image. His solution to this negative publicity was to invite the exile community, as he had done in 1965, to return to the island in order to bring their relatives back with them to the United States. This time the port was Mariel and hence those departing came to be known as "Marielitos." This port became the gateway to the United States for almost 125,000 refugees who arrived in South Florida in the so-called *flotilla de la libertad* (Freedom Flotilla).

On May 5, 1980, President Carter declared: "We'll continue to provide an open heart and open arms to refugees seeking freedom from Communist domination." ("United States Opens Arms to Cuban Exodus," *The Miami Herald* [6 May 1980], 1A). According to the Official Department of State statistics (as they appeared in the Special Report on the 1980 Mariel Exodus), between April 21 and November 2, 1980, 124,779 Cuban refugees arrived in the United States. In spite of an intervening United States order on May 14 to interrupt the boatlift, approximately 87,000 Cubans arrived during that month alone. The numbers gradually began to decrease until only 10 arrivals were reported between October and November 1980. With the intent to discredit the Mariel refugees and to embarrass the Carter administration, the Cuban government added a group of those they considered "undesirables" and "antisocial" to the refugees from the

Peruvian embassy and others who were relatives of United States residents. It is impossible to know the exact number of mentally ill patients, common prisoners, and even lepers Castro included. Most statistics estimate that 300 "undesirables" came to the United States in the Mariel boatlift. Other sources report 300 mental health patients taken from psychiatric hospitals and about 350 common prisoners removed from Cuban jails ("The Mariel Injustice," *The Commission Pro-Justice Mariel Prisoners*. Coral Gables, FL, 1987). Witnesses in Cuba reported that when their boats were ready to leave, the government would force them to take some strangers into their vessels. This gave credibility to the claims that those leaving the island were the *escoria*, the "scum" of society. Upon arrival into the United States, these cases were detected ("FBI Discovering Some Undesirables Among Flood of Refugees from Cuba," *The Washington Post* [29 April 1980], A1; "Some Refugees Suffer Psychological Problems," *The Miami Herald* [17 May 1980], 1C).

Who Were the Marielitos?

There has been much speculation about the Marielitos. One outstanding feature is that many of those who came via Mariel have darker skin than those who fled Cuba in the 1960s. A political factor that goes unnoticed is that previously the government had routinely denied any black or young Cuban permission to leave the island. Earlier it was much easier for older and sick people to obtain permits to come to the United States. When the Port of Mariel opened, it became possible for the first time for many young men and blacks to leave without any legal or formal application. Since the Castro revolution had been predicated upon the principle of liberation especially for the young and Afro-Cubans, the Mariel exodus appeared to compromise those claims.

The appearance of this new group in an already complex and diverse South Florida forced the local community, particularly the Cubans, to respond creatively. Did the Marielitos have a different culture? Were they the same type of Cuban as those who had come to the United States twenty years earlier? Could they possibly fit into the local Cuban community? Would they be able to function in the United States after so many years under communist rule?

One of the most confusing variables during this initial period was the unfortunate literal translation of the word *criminal*. The English language calls criminal anyone who breaks the law, despite the type of offense committed. In Spanish, however, the word *criminal* carries the connotation of a blood crime, a serious offense. Usually when someone commits petty thievery, or any other lesser offense, Hispanics call it a *delito*. Sadly, English translates both concepts with the same word: criminal. Thus, it was this stronger term that the Cuban exile population heard on the airwaves, although the vast majority of those who had broken laws had committed only misdemeanors. This added to the already confusing and painful situation of the Mariel arrival in South Florida. Therefore, at first there was fear and apprehension within the local community. Thankfully, most overcame this fear and an outpouring of volunteers began to help in the crisis caused by the large numbers who arrived each day.

No reflection on the Marielitos would be complete without mentioning the suffering that they endured before and after arriving in the United States. Prior to their departure from Cuba, those who had been in the Peruvian embassy received assurances of their safety while they waited to leave the island. Nonetheless, they were then subjected to insults, ridicule, and even physical abuse. In some instances, government-directed mobs made the refugees march through the streets with derogatory signs hung around their necks. (*Diario Las Américas* [22 May 1980], 10; *The Miami Herald* [23 May 1980], 28A, and 18 May 1980, 24A). These already frightened and traumatized people traveled the 90 miles to Key West where they were welcomed and offered food and attention, but where the living conditions remained difficult. The first days of their stay in South Florida were spent in tent cities and stadiums with no privacy and limited sanitation. It was extremely sad for those who visited Key West in search of relatives and loved ones. Some of the most moving stories tell of confused elderly and helpless women and children feeling lost in this new, chaotic setting. It was common for those who visited the holding center to receive from the Marielitos scraps of paper with the names of relatives or acquaintances who lived in Miami with the plea, "Please tell them we are here!"

One woman arrived in Key West searching for her sister, her brother-in-law, and their child, only to discover that they had been relocated to a detention center in Atlanta. The bus carrying her family had left just minutes before she arrived to claim them. After many telephone calls and desperate efforts, she finally contacted her family.

The tale of the subsequent encounter between this woman and her relatives through the fences of a detention area was both painful and humiliating. Like many others, they had committed no crime other than to arrive in Miami in the midst of a human avalanche for which the city was not prepared. Although most Mariel refugees were processed there and at Key West, others were sent to military bases in Puerto Rico, Arkansas, and all over the United States.

This illustrates the seriousness of the Mariel crisis in South Florida that prompted the subsequent takeover of the refugee reception program by the federal government. Initially, all relief efforts had been in the hands of local agencies and volunteers. The Federal Emergency Management Agency (FEMA) then began to direct the influx of refugees. Although the local services had not been sufficient, they had done a superb job providing food and clothing through thousands of volunteer hours. FEMA, on the other hand, dealt expeditiously with the crisis by transferring the refugees to Eglin Air Force Base in northern Florida and other military bases under their supervision. However, as they were transferred, no attempt was made (at the Key West arrival point) to group them by similarity of background. Thus, many families who arrived together were later actually separated. As a result of this and other factors, a pattern of riots developed in those "storage" sites (Clark et al., 6).

Pastoral Care of the Marielitos

The Catholic Church in South Florida quickly felt the impact of the new arrivals. After the first emergency services of the most basic nature, a variety of initiatives started in an attempt to respond more systematically to the challenges of the Marielito influx. One effort, supervised by the Most Reverend Agustín Román, Auxiliary Bishop of Miami, was the publication of a pamphlet directed to the refugees which offered them guidance and orientation. These simple booklets, prepared by the various Hispanic Apostolic Movements, were widely distributed gratis by lay ministers and women religious.

The presence of the Marielitos in Miami stretched the local church to its most creative peaks. Regional ordained and lay ministers, even Cubans, were not prepared to receive such a massive number of refugees who presented such new pastoral challenges. The Marielitos, especially the young, had been raised in a society where the main concern was daily survival and where personal decisions and initiative were not encouraged. A common cultural conflict centered on the issue of theft. Survival in Cuba had sometimes required petty thievery from the government and there was no moral connotation attached to it. To jump from that standpoint to the legalism that considered any theft unjustified posed a dramatic shift in values for the newly arrived. Moreover, the idea of freedom of choice was foreign to most of them. A consumeristic society often overwhelmed many with daily individual options. Often the Marielitos simply tried to please everyone. Therefore, it was hard to know when they were truly agreeing with something or someone.

Among the most important values of the Marielitos were their love for the extended family and the desire to have their children receive a good education. In Cuba, children were taken from their homes every week and educated in schools with no parental supervision or involvement. For many, this government-controlled education contradicted their religious beliefs. They had risked their lives to come to the United States looking for an alternate way to educate their children. Numerous new refugees were very interested in Christianity and some had been lay ministers in Cuba. They had finally decided to leave the island for religious freedom and educational opportunities for their children. Others had a very limited understanding of the faith. Organized catechetical programs were not effective at first because of a lack of transportation and the Marielitos' unfamiliarity with formal religion classes.

In the Archdiocese of Miami, the pastoral care of the Marielitos took two distinct directions. First, there was the obvious need to deal with those refugees settling in South Florida. Although many had located in New Jersey and California where established Cuban communities existed, most chose to stay with relatives or friends in the Miami area. Second, the archdiocese became the "central switchboard" for communications between those held in detention centers all over the country and their families who often did not even know that they had arrived. The office of Bishop Román received thousands of letters asking, "Where is my mother? Where is my sister? I am sending you their names. Please, Bishop, find them!"

To respond to the needs, local agencies joined efforts and shared resources. Catholic Community Services of the Archdiocese of Miami offered weekly sessions to assist the Marielitos to become acclimated to their new home. Physicians, police officers, psychologists, and other professionals dialogued with them and tried to answer their many questions. The Shrine of Our Lady of Charity, patroness of Cuba, located in Miami, became the spiritual refuge of countless Marielitos (Tweed, Thomas A., *Our Lady of the Exile: Diaspora Religion at a Cuban Catholic Shrine in Miami*. Oxford: Oxford University Press, 1997). There, Bishop Román and the Daughters of Charity cared for the material and spiritual needs of those seeking assistance.

In July of 1981, the Office of Lay Ministry of the Archdiocese of Miami began an outreach program to Cubans and other Hispanics in the Hialeah area. St. John the Apostle parish was chosen to pilot this initiative because of its large Marielito population. The many pastoral needs identified during a home visitation program led to the establishment of the *Centro Católico de Evangelización* (Catholic Evangelization Center) in Hialeah. This effort of the Office of Lay Ministry was financed by the Pallotine Fathers and other charitable foundations. The center served as a storefront church for thousands of Marielitos. The permanent deacon and the lay ministers coordinating the ministry experienced firsthand the struggles of the early Marielitos.

For example, a fourteen-year-old boy arrived with his father, a former political prisoner in Cuba, his mother, and his sister. Shortly after, his father died of cancer in Miami. Despite all the suffering, today this young man is a professional, active member of the local community, happily married and with a young family.

The Mariel journey was long and painful, but within a year they already recounted successes. Marielitos did not only receive. Evelio Taillacq, a writer with *Exito* magazine, explains that "the contributions made by Marielitos to the greater Cuban community are immeasurable, particularly in the arts. They have reestablished cultural ties in reminding (the Cuban community) where they come from (quoted by Fernando Trulin IV, "Marielito Success Reinvigorates United States Cuban Community," *Hispanic Link Weekly Report* [18 February 1996]). Among the Marielitos today are private entrepreneurs, successful business executives, realtors, television producers, radio broadcasters, and a great number of church ministers.

Many families were reunited through the Mariel boatlift. Blacks, young people, and others who had been unable to leave Cuba legally during the prior exodus found at last a way to meet their loved ones in exile. Others, however, found it more difficult to adjust to life in the United States.

The Mariel Prisoners

The story of what is known as the Mariel Injustice, recounted in the document by the same name, is one of the most painful realities of the period. There were approximately 2,800 Mariel refugees who, after arriving in the United States, and in some cases after settling with their families and holding jobs, committed crimes. Eighty percent of these offenses were misdemeanors, and the defendants received short sentences ("The Mariel Injustice," 10). After serving their time, instead of being released, they were sent to the maximum security penitentiary in Atlanta. The harshness of the Atlanta Penitentiary made many despair: By 1987, there had been eight suicides and four hundred suicide attempts. The cases of self-inflicted mutilations were also numerous ("The Mariel Injustice," 14). The unjust detention of many Marielitos prompted ongoing advocacy efforts from the Archdiocese of Miami and other agencies and community groups. When President Reagan visited Miami on July 23, 1986, archdiocesan leaders wrote him a letter later published by a local newspaper. The Most Reverend Edward A. McCarthy, then Archbishop of Miami, the Most Reverend Agustín Román, Auxiliary Bishop, and the Reverend Monsignor Bryan O. Walsh, Director of Catholic Community Services, all signed it. The three religious leaders asked for the President's attention to six serious matters. The fourth of these was a request to help the Mariel prisoners in the Atlanta Penitentiary, especially those who had never committed a crime in Cuba or in the United States. The letter asked for an independent tribunal to process each case individually. ("Carta de la Arquidiócesis de Miami al Presidente de los Estados Unidos," *Diario Las Américas* [25 July 1986]).

In April 1986, the Subcommittee on the Administration of Justice of the House Committee on the Judiciary had identified 1,929 Cubans incarcerated in the Federal Penitentiary in Atlanta who were not serving criminal sentences. They comprised at least four distinguishable groups. First were those suffering from mental illness. The second included persons who never received entry permits to this country because they had committed serious crimes in Cuba. The third group were those who, upon arrival, were granted parole and subsequently committed crimes here and were serving their sentences.

It was the fourth group that caused and today still causes anger in everyone who values justice. This group, having served their sentences for minor crimes committed in this country, remained imprisoned. Committing a crime after arriving in the United States constituted a violation of parole, thus making them subject to deportation. However, in their case, the Cuban government refused to take them back, making deportation impossible. This resulted in indefinite imprisonment, sometimes for petty thievery or for driving under the influence of alcohol.

The above information was reported in a November 1987 joint statement by the Most Reverend Agustín Román of Miami and the late Most Reverend Enrique San Pedro, S.J., then auxiliary bishop of Galveston-Houston, Texas. Also in November of 1987, Bishop Román presented the National Conference of Catholic Bishops with a list of nearly 700 Mariel refugees who had completed their sentences but remained in prison. Román pleaded for the prisoners' release to relatives willing to accept the responsibility.

As time passed and nothing was accomplished, many United States officials, politicians, and public personalities joined the plea for the fair treatment of the prisoners. Cases such as the Cuban mother held in prison with her husband because three years earlier they had both pleaded guilty to possessing an ounce of marijuana made headlines all over the country. Their two small children were being given up for adoption by social workers because they did not know how long the parents would remain in prison. Many began to call the Mariel prisoners "pawns" in the political game between Castro and the United States.

The 1987 Prison Riots in Oakdale and Atlanta

Frustration, despair, and hopelessness escalated. In November of 1987, the Cuban government agreed to take back about 2,700 Cubans who had come in the Mariel boatlift. Bishop Román declared that "the deportation of Mariel prisoners who had already served their sentences in the United States was a violation of human rights" ("The Mariel Injustice," 186). The threat of deportation and a subsequent life sentence in Cuban prisons prompted riots in Oakdale, Louisiana, and Atlanta, Georgia. Saturday, November 21, inmates rampaged through the Oakdale compound overpowering guards. Several people were injured and twenty-eight hostages were taken. In Atlanta, one inmate died and fires erupted in several buildings. Negotiations began at both sites, but no resolution appeared imminent. The Mariel inmates had decided to die rather than to return to Cuba. On November 23, detainees at Oakdale asked to meet with Bishop Román. Known as a strong advocate for their cause, he had gained their trust and respect. On November 28, Oakdale inmates posted banners blaming officials for the breakdown in negotiations and demanding that Bishop Román participate in the talks. Sunday, November 29, a videotaped appeal by Román was repeatedly viewed by Oakdale detainees. When the Bishop arrived at that prison, the inmates threw down their weapons and began releasing hostages. On Wednesday, December 2, the Atlanta inmates met with a Legal Aid lawyer and heard the taped appeal from Bishop Román. Negotiators and inmate representatives signed an agreement in his presence. As a result, all the Atlanta hostages were released. The crisis had ended, but the injustice continued.

On January 28, 1988, Cuban civic organizations in exile, with the encouragement of Bishop Román, gathered in Miami to establish a Task Force formed by lawyers, businesspersons, and community leaders. The Task Force would continue to work on issues related to the legal situation of the Mariel prisoners. As a result of their work, more than 3,700 inmates, after paying their debt to society, were released and are now reunited with their families and are completely integrated into society. The Task Force later confirmed that those former Mariel prisoners have one of the lowest rates of repeat offenses in the United States. ("Task Force apela al Departamento de Justicia para que se detengan deportaciones hacia Cuba," *Diario Las Américas* [10 February 1990]).

In February 1998, a spokesperson from the office of Senator Bob Graham informed the Office of Lay Ministry of the Archdiocese of Miami that since 1984, 1,371 Marielitos had been deported to Cuba. The Senator also reported that in 1998 there were still 1,665 Mariel refugees in custody. A local Cuban lawyer told a representative of the Office of Lay Ministry that approximately 1,200 of those still detained are part of that group suffering indefinite and therefore unjust imprisonment.

A Personal Note

The joys and the hopes, the griefs and the anxieties of the people of this age, especially those who are

poor or in any way afflicted, these too, are the joys
and hopes, the griefs and anxieties of the followers
of Christ. (*Gaudium et Spes* #1)

Writing this chapter on the Marielito experience has allowed me to
witness once more the greatness and the smallness of humanity. I have
heard stories of courage and self-giving interwoven with those of
cowardice and selfishness. The openness of many to tell me their
stories and to make accessible to me their resources fills me with hope
and gratitude. The attempt on the part of others to minimize or
trivialize the impact of so much suffering in our community makes
me feel helpless. The Mariel boatlift was unique in the sense that it
was massive and sudden, and the community was not in any way
prepared for it. Yet, after that period, South Florida has continued to
witness the arrival of the *balseros* (rafters) who take to the sea from
Cuba on anything that floats in an attempt to reach the United States.
Some have made it; others have lost their lives.

Most recently, the local church responded to the *Guantanamo*
crisis and the influx of those new refugees with perhaps a better
organized and more efficiently executed relief effort. This was possible
in part because of the confidence and competence gained from the
Mariel experience.

But underneath every exodus is the same pain, the same suffering,
the same despair. The Mariel migration is another chapter in the
history of people's inhumanity to people; it offered a fresh opportunity for the church to open her arms to the joys and the grief of the
people of this age. As we approach the new millennium, there are still
people living in detention centers for no reason other than having
been caught in the game of politics. The Mariel boatlift is over, but
the arrival in the United States of refugees and immigrants from all
parts of the world continues. The search for better living conditions,
freedom, and economic opportunities goes on. For many, who see the
United States as the promised land, the church may be the only hope.

Conclusion: The Future of the Marielito Ministry

The church's ministry to Marielitos can be improved. Some needs
and concerns still requiring attention as we enter a new millennium
are:
1. As of February 13, 1998, approximately 1,200 Mariel prisoners

were still suffering indefinite, unfair detention. Efforts need to continue and to expand in order to bring justice to these people who have been in detention centers for years despite completing their sentences.

2. In many cases, these prisoners have been separated for years from their families. Parishes are beginning to respond to this crisis by identifying and reaching out to those within their parochial boundaries who find themselves in this painful limbo. Such family ministry must be intensified.

3. The early Cuban exodus in the 1960s was marked by the rise and growth of the apostolic movements, primarily *Cursillo*. Two main factors caused this phenomenon: local parishes did not welcome the new arrivals in ways that were culturally sensitive, and most of the Cubans were not active in the American parish system because it was foreign to them. Because the parishes did not meet their needs, ministry to the new arrivals was done mostly through the Catholic Welfare Bureau and the apostolic movements. Although those movements have developed and now advocate parish involvement, for many Mariel families the parish system remains irrelevant. Home visitation programs and other outreach efforts need to continue.

4. Marielitos, especially the young, lived for twenty years in a communist regime. During this time they developed a mistrust for any institution and perceived the church as persecuted and poor. The newly arrived, however, encountered a different kind of church in the United States. This church was influential. It owned schools, hospitals, beautiful churches, and offices. It offered welfare programs and legal aid. Simply put, this new church enjoyed political and economic power.

I personally know Marielitos who had been active Catholics in Cuba. Yet, after two years in Miami, they had embraced all the questionable ideals of mainline America: consumerism, materialism and individualism. Ministry among them, as among any other immigrant group, needs to model a servant church, that is, a community of disciples who walks alongside the poor and the oppressed in imitation of the poor Christ. Our church must always use its power for the poor and model the servitude of Jesus.

THE PASTORAL CARE OF THE PUERTO RICAN WOMAN IN THE UNITED STATES

Irma S. Corretjer-Nolla

Introduction

Although *Puertorriqueñas* (Puerto Rican women) were present in the United States before the twentieth century, the history of their pastoral care in this country is just beginning. Their presence contributes to the 30 million Hispanics in the country who make up the 39% of the Catholic Church and are predicted to be over 50% of the church by 2010 (Secretariat for Hispanic Affairs of the National Catholic Conference of Bishops). At the end of this millennium, there is a vast number of Catholic *Puertorriqueñas* in the United States with different social, economic, and educational backgrounds. Most of them are bilingual and bicultural. There are social and historical elements that set them apart from other Hispanic women. To provide proper and effective pastoral care, one must understand their unique history and their life experience. This chapter therefore deals with: 1) Puerto Rican Migrations to the United States; 2) Citizenship and Its Effects; 3) Puerto Rican Women; 4) The Lay Apostolate and Pastoral Care in Rural Puerto Rico; 5) What We Mean by Pastoral Care; 6) Modern Challenges to Pastoral Care Providers; 7) *Puertorriqueñas* at the End of the Century; 8) The Military Environment; 9) Military Women and Wives; 10) Puerto Rican Leadership in the Military Parish and Civilian Community; 11) Poverty and Unmarried Mothers: Pastoral Concerns. Facing these factors should encourage the pastoral ministers in the Catholic Church, and society in general, to discover, nurture, and support the hidden wealth of Puerto Rican women in the United States.

Puerto Rican Migrations to the United States

The annexation of Puerto Rico as a new territory to the United States after the 1898 war brought an abrupt break in the Spanish political and religious history of the island and inevitable socioeconomic effects to its people. Since great poverty had previously prevailed, for many the United States presence quickly became a symbol of hope.

In *El Emigrante Puertorriqueño* (Rio Piedras, Puerto Rico, 1987), Luis Nieves Falcón describes how the new government sought to improve the economy by encouraging large emigrations from the island to work farms in Hawaii, California, and Arizona or textile industries in New Jersey and New York. After World War I, New York City became a more accessible port of entry for Puerto Ricans. Therefore, many settled there. During the early 1950s there was a massive Puerto Rican immigration into the United States. Over 600,000 left the island for economic, political, and military reasons (Korea). This increased the Puerto Rican population in the mainland to over one million. Today, at 2.7 million in the United States, we are the second largest Hispanic group. We affect not only society (e.g., schools), but have an even greater influence on today's church.

To travel and study in the United States had not been unusual for the Puerto Rican elites of the nineteenth century. But the new immigration made the Puerto Rican presence obvious, a trend which continues. Today, Puerto Ricans are in every state of the union. Among the areas of major concentration are Chicago, Philadelphia, the northern and eastern part of Virginia, and in the northeastern states. Another smaller but constant migration is from these northeastern states and from the island to cities such as Orlando, Tampa, Jacksonville, Miami, San Antonio, Houston, and Denver. These latter are migrations especially of professionals and retired military (1996 Unpublished Diocesan Hispanic Ministry Survey, Mexican American Cultural Center, San Antonio, TX; 1995 United States Census Bureau; 1997 Unpublished National Survey by the author).

Citizenship and Its Effects

In 1917 the United States Congress granted citizenship to the Puerto Rican people. This set us apart from the immigrant Hispanic community in the United States. Puerto Ricans were subjected to the provisions of the Selective Service Act and therefore to the draft. Mexican Americans as United States citizens are also subject to the draft, but they are not an immigrant community. Consequently, although Hispanics make up only 6.4% of the active military (*Chicago Tribune*, 19 April 1998), Puerto Ricans have been the largest Hispanic group born outside the mainland to serve in the United States Armed Forces.

World War I found Puerto Ricans fighting and dying for North American ideals. The military draft brought new Puerto Rican immigrants and their families to the mainland. By World War II, several military installations were established on the island. Many of our local young women married American military men, left the island, and settled in the United States.

It was in 1957 that I became a part of these statistics when I accompanied my husband who had joined the military service. Like the hopeful Puerto Ricans during the United States invasion of the last century, I felt that to be part of the Armed Forces was an accomplishment and a great opportunity for the future. Triumphant Hollywood World War II movies, and what we heard from military persons returning to the island, contributed to our deep and proud sense of American patriotism. To be part of the military was the route to serve our "country" and to move up in the world. This new life was also the opening to a pluralistic world; we came to know other countries, cultures, and languages. As a young Puerto Rican woman, wife, and mother seeking and hoping for a better life, joining the military and leaving the island seemed good. Unfortunately, I soon discovered that we Puerto Ricans are different; most of us will miss our small island forever.

Puerto Rican Women

Who are these women who became United States citizens and later residents of the continental United States? Puerto Rican historians, sociologists, and feminists agree that it is important to understand the traditional patterns of socialization transmitted from one generation to another. They have affected and molded the Puerto Rican woman's role in the family, society, and the church.

The clash between the Taíno indigenous civilization and the European conquerors produced a paradox reflected in Puerto Rican women ever since. Edna Acosta Colón described the social role of Taíno women:

The most recent works we researched document the fact that the tradition of the matrilineal family structure was one of the principal characteristics of the culture of the Taíno, the original tribe to inhabit what is today Puerto Rico. In the Taíno social structure, women had access to the highest political office possible, that of chief, attainable by maternal, paternal or matrimonial ties. (*La mujer en la sociedad puertor-riqueña*. Río Piedras, Puerto Rico: Ediciones Huracán, 1980)

Remains of this political power are evident today in the town of Loíza which retained the name of the Taíno woman chieftain who ruled that area. During this century Puerto Rican women such as *Doña* (Mrs.) Felisa Rincón de Gautier, the first elected mayor of San Juan, and its current mayor, *Doña* (Mrs.) Sila Calderón, have wielded political power.

Acosta Colón points out the social and religious equality and responsibility, the value and respect given to the woman in the Taíno society:

. . . inheritance was traced by maternal lines . . . women as well as men in that society bore arms and learned how to use them, which they did, in war. Furthermore, they participated fully in the production of goods and providing services, in religious and other ceremonies.

The Spanish conquest brought other ideas about women to the island. Ours is a history of the sexual exploitation suffered by the Taíno woman and the African slaves imported by the Spaniards. These relationships created children not recognized by their fathers. Their mothers bore total responsibility for them. During the eighteenth and nineteenth centuries the church issued several pastoral letters denouncing the inhumane treatment of these women, and the abuse of the children of this concubinage or common law relationships. These pastorals opposed extramarital relationships, incest, prostitution, and abortion. However, some historians claim that the tone and vocabulary of the pastoral letters did not respond justly to the reality of these women. Their image remained tarnished when held even indirectly responsible for this abuse when, for instance, women are seen tempting men (María F. de Barceló Miller, *De la Polilla a la Virtud: Visión sobre la mujer de la Iglesia Jerárquica de Puerto Rico*. La Mujer en Puerto Rico. Ensayos de Investigación. Edición de Yamila Azize Vargas. Ediciones Huracán, Inc. 1987).

Two centuries of well-intentioned pastoral letters, fines for violations of these pastoral restrictions, opposition to the *fiestas* (popular celebrations considered opportunities for licentiousness), and stern rules concerning some sacraments slowly strained the relationship between the hierarchy and the common people, especially women. Hierarchical opposition to popular religious practices alienated the *campesino* (farm worker) of the interior of the island. Despite opposition, the *campesinos* continued to nurture their faith through these personal and communal celebrations.

> The systematic and perennial submission suffered by the Puerto Rican women, be that of oppression conscious or not, must be traced not from the period of the Taíno, but from the time of the Spaniards' colonization. (Rodriguez Cortés, Sonia. "Socio-Cultural-Religious Background of Puerto Rican Women." *Homines* [Vol. 10, No. 2], 1986–87).

The arrival of white Spanish women to the island, and their role in the life of the colony, occasioned new social class distinctions. First were the newly arrived Spaniards. Second, the *criollo* or white Spaniards born on the island. At the bottom was the rural *jíbaro*. Spanish women established a meaningful family life for their own class. According to Rodriguez Cortés, that life was no different from

> . . . English women of the Victorian period. From childhood they were taught domestic tasks and duties. Their sphere of influence encompassed whatever pertained to husband, home and children. As a member of the group, the Spanish woman was subject to the authority of both father and husband.

During the 1800s the rural jíbaro family unit eked out a subsistence by cultivating its land. The home was the center of daily life. Women participated in the agriculture but were also responsible for cooking, housekeeping, raising and educating the children.

However, the end of that century brought changes in the role of Puerto Rican women in family and society. The island was transformed from a subsistence economy into an exportation industry. This newly developed industrial system gave the *jíbaras* the opportunity to harvest sugar and coffee or work as servants in the *haciendas* (ranches). The family still needed to procure its own sustenance. Consequently, there was little time left after working to care for home responsibilities. Women picking coffee beans, spinning tobacco leaves, or in the needle industry sometimes neglected their homes and children. The quality of life of the *campesino* (farm worker) deteriorated. Such social conflicts caused indices of childhood diseases, mortality, alcoholism, and crime to rise. The church expressed her concern in the *Carta Pastoral que con motivo de la Santa Cuaresma dirige a sus diocesanos el Ilmo. Sr. Don Fray Toribio Miguella y Arnedo, Obispo de Puerto Rico* (Puerto Rico, Imprenta del Boletín Mercantil, 1895. *Archivo Histórico Arquidiocesano*, Arquidiócesis de San Juan).

Bishop Pablo Benigno Carrión provided more personal pastoral care to urban Puerto Rican women when he initiated spiritual retreats. He promoted Marian devotion by comparing Mary's role to women's honorable place in society and family. Undoubtedly, Marian devotion helped to transform the attitudes of the Puerto Rican Church toward women and their role within the family. The Christian family became the clear center of the Puerto Rican society. Nonetheless, the new and important role of women in society was not enough to liberate them from the idea that men were the head of the family (Barceló Miller, p. 74).

The Lay Apostolate and Pastoral Care in Rural Puerto Rico

At the onset of United States colonization, a pastoral phenomenon appeared on the island in response to the rural pastoral needs. The alienated *campesino* had few Catholic clergy but many new American Protestant missionaries. In response, two Catholic laymen known as *Los Hermanos Cheos* initiated an apostolic movement. They preached missions and provided pastoral care other than the sacraments. Their counterpart, *Hermanas Cheas* (rural Puerto Rican women), were of various ages, and civil and social status. They were lay prophets of their times: evangelizing, directing spiritual retreats, and becoming rural community organizers and leaders who built chapels in the countryside.

There is very little written about this remarkable group which was the strength and support of the Catholic Church in difficult times. The Rev. José Dimas Soberal made this subject the topic for his dissertation. Copies of that unpublished historical research are available from the *Centro Arizmendi*, Bayamón, Puerto Rico. A related publication is Rev. Esteban Santaella Rivera's *Historia de Los Her-*

manos Cheos: Recopilación de escritos y relatos (Editora Alfa y Omega, Dominican Republic, 1979).

These rural Puerto Rican women gained for themselves a valuable and recognized place in the Catholic Church. Their dedication reveals the strong apostolic and pastoral potential that lies in the heart of the Puerto Rican woman and demonstrates what she can contribute to the church.

After years of investigation, Bishop Jaime E. McManus, C.S.S.R, Bishop of Ponce, blessed the apostolic effort in 1951, named a spiritual director, and ordered the establishment of a formation center for the "hermanos." Their leadership, initiative, and active participation in evangelization 60 years before the Second Vatican Council were "signs of the times" for the role of the laity, especially women. Today this prophetic lay group continues to evangelize in the rural areas of the island and many serve Hispanics on the mainland. The diocesan director for Hispanic ministry in the diocese of Rochester, New York, comes from the evangelizing experience of the *Hermanos Cheos:* Luis Ruberte is well respected for his preaching and teaching style.

Like many other women in history, *Puertorriqueñas* played an important role in the preservation of the Catholic faith during early emigrations. Like *Las Cheas*, these new immigrant women were mainly from rural areas and showed the same stamina and strength in sharing their faith with the community.

Ana María Díaz-Stevens (*Hispanic Catholic Culture in the United States.* University of Notre Dame Press, 1994) tells of a group of young Puerto Ricans:

> . . . [they] were asked who was the person they most respected in the community aside from their parents. In most cases (66.6%) the person mentioned was an elderly woman in the community known for her piety and her role as the leader of nonecclesiastical religious communal rituals and prayer.

These women were known as *Las rezadoras* (pray-leaders), women with a deep faith and prayer life who transmitted the community's traditions.

What We Mean by Pastoral Care

Pastoral care is the ministry the church provides to its flock in answer to their personal and communal needs. It is mainly provided through parishes. Pastoral care also occurs in the community at large when average parishioners are part of the pastoral activity of the church in service to their community.

A "call to be a compassionate and healing presence toward the other" is how parishioners participating in a diocesan consultation in a Western state described quality pastoral care. It is a way of learning to share and appreciate each other's lives "in joy and pain, struggle and triumph, conversion and new life." People continued to define pastoral care as a:

> ... presence and care to the homebound, sick and dying; the imprisoned; ministry to those in grief because of death, separation, divorce; care of the elderly at home or in nursing homes; pastoral counseling and spiritual direction and presence and care to any other anonymous groups.

Responses to a survey on pastoral care mailed by the author to 30 cities in 13 states during January and February of 1997 revealed that many Puerto Rican women could not identify with the inherent responsibility of the word "pastoral." Some respondents agreed that one function of pastoral care is the spiritual or emotional support given within church structures. However, others did not see themselves as pastoral care providers or in need of such care. One third did not respond.

Undoubtedly, the understanding of pastoral care varies according to personal and parish life experiences, formal education, and formation in faith and church concerns. The term may be confusing to many and misunderstood by some. Most times pastoral care is associated with the obligations of the hierarchy.

Modern Challenges to Pastoral Care Providers

In a telephone conversation Alicia Rivera, former coordinator of the Hispanic Family Life Office in the Archdiocese of Chicago, said that many Puerto Rican women in that city are "strong pillars of faith and achievers in their communities." Her statement reiterates the important role of *Puertorriqueñas* in the life of the Catholic Church, not only in Chicago, but throughout the United States. Alicia recalled how these women have earned the respect of the Chicago Catholic community by developing, strengthening, and helping the diaconate program. They epitomize Puerto Rican women's strength in times of social/cultural change and deep spiritual needs.

Other Puerto Rican women who work in diocesan Hispanic ministry or apostolates throughout the nation spoke with pride about the many *Puertorriqueñas* active in their Catholic communities and the significance of their leadership. A common element is the spiritual growth and conversion experienced through their participation in some apostolic movements, especially the *Cursillos de Cristiandad* (short courses in Christianity). Conversion is the common denominator among these women both on the island and the mainland.

On the other hand, most of the diocesan leaders in Hispanic ministry observed that many Puerto Ricans who come to church yet remain inactive in parish life have not lived through a conversion experience or formation similar to these others. The Catholic Puerto Rican community comprises both those who are truly committed to the pastoral care of the church and a large number who remain on the periphery. Occasionally those on the margins come to church, but they will not commit themselves to provide pastoral care. However, when in need of help themselves, they might be the first to look for it in the church community. So *Puertorriqueñas* find themselves on both sides of pastoral care. The majority are in need, but there are also many who provide pastoral care to others.

These thoughts are reaffirmed in my survey. Ninety-four percent of the respondents are Catholic women, of whom 70% attend church weekly. Seventy-seven percent are registered parishioners, of whom only 40% say they do not participate in any pastoral activity. Of those who are active, 20% serve one hour or less a month; 19% give two to four hours of service; 20% serve five or more hours a month in their parish. Of those serving two to four hours a month, most said they had undergone a conversion experience in an apostolic movement or a retreat in the Catholic Church.

Puertorriqueñas at the End of the Century

Second- and third-generation Puerto Rican women emerge like a Phoenix from the ashes of previous migrations. Despite the 1990 Census Bureau statistics that show that *Puertorriqueñas* are disproportionately single mothers, divorced, and poor, we find today that many of them also enjoy the accomplishments of higher education and better professional job opportunities. On this subject I was pleasantly surprised by the answers to my pastoral care survey. Almost all the women who answered had attended either high school, vocational or business school. Approximately 33% of them have had some college. Thirty-eight percent have bachelors degrees, 18% have completed master's degrees or postgraduate courses, and 3% hold doctorates.

Puerto Rican women in the United States are in many professional fields including government, law, politics, sciences, arts, and theater. They influence the entire Hispanic/Latino community, even all facets of the greater American community.

From my experience at the national, regional, and diocesan level, I feel comfortable stating that the Catholic diocesan Hispanic ministry or apostolate throughout the nation is supported and strengthened by many Puerto Rican lay and religious women. They occupy church positions at the national, diocesan, and parish levels, and generously share the richness of their Catholic faith. Dedicated examples include Sally Gómez-Kelley and Sisters Verónica Méndez and Dominga Zapata.

The Military Environment

Puerto Ricans migrate mainly for economic reasons, but also to fulfill their military obligation. Service in the Armed Forces is not a major reason other Hispanic/Latino groups emigrate to the United States, although quite often they use it as a step toward legal residence and eventual citizenship. Thus, in recent years there has been an increase of Panamanians, Peruvians, Colombians, and Cubans on military active duty. Many of them are children of Hispanic immigrants. Even those not born in the United States are usually citizens now. As a Puerto Rican military wife expressed it, "We are all part of the same family." Consequently, the composition of the Hispanic military community has changed since I was a military wife years ago. However, the pastoral needs are the same, although on a larger scale.

Active duty Puerto Rican military families and retirees who reside near military installations need planned and effective pastoral care. Like civilian Hispanic communities, these parishioners lack Spanish-speaking clergy. Therefore, established lay leadership that is knowledgeable and sensitive to the military environment is essential.

However, the constant movement of the active military makes it difficult to organize well-formed lay leadership among them. Consequently, the retired military communities offer a tremendous opportunity for pastoral formation and commitment. They can provide pastoral care continuity to military parish life.

Military Women and Wives

In my 1997 survey, 34% of married women came to the United States with their military husbands and 3% with their military parents. These are numbers which cannot be ignored. The Puerto Rican military wives came from different economical, social, and educational backgrounds.

As military women and military wives, they have experienced the insecurities and terrors of war. They have known the fear of going to bed unsure what tomorrow holds: Will they see the dawn? Will they wake up widows? These women have known the loneliness of raising a family while their husbands were away at war or on temporary duties. They have moved with the entire family to strange new places every two to four years. Therefore, these women have to be the emotional and spiritual balance for their children's transitions and the stress of these migrant experiences. Many of them suffer cultural and linguistic alienation. But it would be a mistake to pity them. These are women who have clung together even in difficult or violent times. They have strengthened each other in faith, prayer, and care. Some of them hold leadership roles and are strong models for the others to follow. Military women and wives are an uncommon breed; they are survivors!

In the Military Ordinariate records, Puerto Ricans and Hispanic families are not classified according to their ethnic groups. There is no perceived need to identify the differences of culture and language among the minority groups within the military. No consideration is given to appropriate evangelization, catechesis, or the need for the sacraments in their own language much less any pastoral planning that responds to their cultural needs.

Bishop José de Jesús Madera, Vicar for Hispanics in the Military, told me in a telephone interview that most Puerto Rican women find spiritual and emotional support in small groups of other Puerto Rican friends. The closeness of these gatherings becomes their home away from home. Bishop Madera questions why *Puertorriqueñas* do not join other groups, in particular, the Military Council of Catholic Women. Most of them remain removed from the community at large in deference to their small groups of friends. For many, parish life and pastoral participation is practically nonexistent. The Bishop's comment was a reminder of Puerto Rican women of earlier centuries and their alienation from the institutional church.

Several military wives I surveyed said that they and their families do not feel welcome in their church. Some mentioned lifeless liturgies which held no meaning for them. Consequently, they preferred to withdraw from military parish life.

I remember our first assignment outside Puerto Rico in 1957. At every Sunday mass, I felt that I was a stranger. The English homily had no meaning for me. I followed the mass from my Spanish missal. My most difficult time was confession. I used to confess weekly in preparation for Sunday communion. I prepared an examination of conscience which looked more like a shopping list than a spiritual step for deeper conversion. In the darkness of the confessional, I tried to read with my best English pronunciation what I felt had been my failings. Most of the time I was successful. Other times the priest asked questions which I hardly understood and was less able to answer. My most traumatic experience was when the priest yelled and left me in a state of shock. I did not know what he was saying or what I had said. It was the most painful Easter Triduum of my life. I could not complete my penance. I did not know if I had been forgiven. I went to communion thinking that, if I were committing a sacrilege, I needed God's mercy more than ever. It was only my Catholic education and strong formation that helped me persevere and continue to attend mass in that strange and cold community.

Culture and language are barriers to the spiritual and pastoral care of military families, especially the women, since they are the bearers of culture. Cultural differences create a void in the emotional and spiritual care of the Hispanic military community. The Hispanic military family is no different from the civilian one. Their identity and dignity demand and deserve recognition, consideration, and above all, respect.

During our 23 years as a military family, our house was home to many other military men, women, and dependents. It was most home when we heard, *"Bendición, Papi y Mami"* (Bless me, Papa and Mama), as they came into the house. This is a request for a blessing from the mother and/or the father or from anyone older. It is a tradition learned in Puerto Rican homes. The response is, *"Que Dios te bendiga y la Virgen te acompañe"* (May God bless you and the Blessed Mother be with you).

The pastoral care in our military home fulfilled their spiritual, social, and often financial needs. It lent a sense of belonging, of home to the lonely, the young, the women, the couple, and the family. We saw several return to the practice of their Catholic faith. What I thought at the time was unique to our family, I later realized was a cultural and traditional practice among Puerto Ricans (Juarez-Palma, N. "Pastoral Care to Hispanic Military Families." *Military Chaplain Review* [Summer 1992]). A great value of the Puerto Rican is hospitality, the natural expression of concern and care for each other. However, most are not aware that such actions are the beginning of what is meant by pastoral care. They do not associate it with Christian action. For the majority, it is simply a way of life. Are they conscious that they are the church?

The sense of community embedded in the Puerto Rican psyche is historically idiosyncratic. The island's size, topography, the isolated towns in the mountainous center, and the social establishment of the *hacendados* (self-sufficient ranches) forced people to be a community. Therefore, our history taught us to be a festive, hospitable, and communitarian people. This was reaffirmed by Bishop Madera's comment about our community or cluster behavior, our need for close relationships, and our tremendous hospitality.

The church document, *Evangelii Nuntiandi*, clarifies these natural feelings and ways of thinking. The evangelization of:

> . . . a culture and cultures, in the wide and rich sense which these terms have in *Gaudium et Spes*, always takes the person as one's starting point and always comes back to the relationships of people among themselves and with God.

It is their culture that brings Puerto Ricans together. Pastoral care can build on this natural concern for each other. Eventually a deeper conversion may occur as people are nurtured by their faith relationship with God. Proper pastoral care of the Puerto Rican community can help develop a true sense of being the church through small communities that support their Catholic faith and empower them to serve.

Puerto Rican Leadership in the Military Parish and Civilian Community

During the last decade, I have perceived an increase in the active participation of the Hispanic community in the military parish. I believe this is due primarily to the effort of formed and informed lay leadership. *The National Pastoral Plan for Hispanic Ministry* (NPPHM) was an instrument that helped the Hispanic community to understand better their pastoral needs and responsibilities. It made official the conclusions of the third national meeting (*III Encuentro*) of the United States Hispanic Catholics. The NPPHM (Secretariat for Hispanic Affairs, NCCB/USCC, 1987) specifically mentioned the military in the Missionary Option, Article #59:

> Meetings of military chaplains according to areas where there are Hispanic personnel. The objective is to: 1) Integrate the process of the III Encuentro in their specific ministry, 2) reflect together on the situation of Hispanics in the military, especially women, given the difficulties and pressures which they frequently encounter, 3) elaborate a program of conscientization and evangelization for Hispanics in the military.

Many chaplains are unaware that such a plan exists. Most of them were not part of the III Encuentro Process or familiar with the pastoral response of the many diocesan offices for Hispanic ministry. Sometimes this ignorance contributes to the oversight of the particular pastoral needs not only of the Puerto Rican, but of the entire Hispanic military community.

However, sometimes lay leaders are welcomed by the non-Hispanic chaplains. If chaplains are sensitive to culture and language differences, as was the case in Ft. McClellan in Alabama in 1990–93, then many Hispanic women flourish and provide pastoral care.

Ada, a Puerto Rican military wife, is a good example. She discovered two confinement centers for women near her new assignment. After several months of asking, she finally was allowed to visit the prison and brought reading materials, especially bibles. Today she brings communion, conducts bible studies, and shares spiritual reflections. She is a positive influence in the lives of this group of primarily Mexican women. Ada is a church leader who uses her bilingual and bicultural talents and catechetical knowledge in the pastoral care of the incarcerated. The women prisoners trust her and accept her advice and guidance because she is often present with the Spanish-speaking priest who visits every other month. There are many Puerto Rican women like Ada, capable and committed to the pastoral care of others both in the civilian and the military communities. In most of the cases it is to the advantage of the local church to encourage these women in their pastoral activities.

"The presence of the military wife or woman and her influence wherever she is found cannot be ignored," said Salvadoran Elisa Montalvo, the diocesan director for Hispanic ministry in Richmond, Virginia. Elisa confirms that her local church enjoys the special energy brought by the Puerto Rican military wives from the Virginia Beach Naval and Air Force military bases. This is evident in the vibrant organization and participation in the pastoral care at both the parish and diocesan level.

Poverty and Unmarried Mothers: Pastoral Concerns

As mentioned earlier, a painful reality peculiar to Puerto Ricans in the United States is their poverty. The 1993 updates of the United States Census Bureau statistics showed that Hispanic/Latino families in the United States have a poverty rate of 27%, more than twice the national average. Puerto Ricans make up 35% of that Hispanic poverty. Of the Puerto Ricans, almost three quarters are single women. The second largest Hispanic group in the United States is unfortunately also the poorest.

Another pastoral challenge to the church is the numerous births to unmarried mothers. Births to single mothers are 25.3% for the general population, but 53% for Puerto Rican women. For the church, this is a "call to be compassionate"; to assist, encourage, and educate the unmarried and impoverished Puerto Rican woman. Could this be another opportunity for the many well-educated Puerto Rican women to serve the church as a catalyst in their own community?

Conclusion

The NPPHM specifically mentioned the needs of the poor and women in the military. In 1987 these concerns were evident; today they are urgent. Continued research of Puerto Rican reality throughout the nation, especially of the capable, valuable women who are making a difference in our communities, is essential for our Church.

The pastoral needs of Puerto Rican women are no different from other women. They are human beings created by God with basic needs: to belong, to learn, to share, to love, and to celebrate. Moreover, the bicultural and bilingual Puerto Rican women and their leadership are valuable pastoral instruments in the multicultural and military parish in the United States. If given pastoral formation and an opportunity to serve, these women can enrich any Catholic community. It is true that there are specific needs among the divorced single parent and poor Puerto Rican women. But I believe that we have the potential and capacity to serve each other. Like the Puerto Rican woman of the early immigrations, we are called to be evangelizers. As *Las Cheas* and *las rezadoras* for the new millennium, we must care for and protect our Catholic faith, witness to our church communities, and offer strength, leadership, and pastoral care to the most needy.

SEVEN TIPS ON THE PASTORAL CARE OF UNITED STATES CATHOLICS OF MEXICAN DESCENT

Eduardo C. Fernández, S.J.

Recently I was taken aback when a friend of mine, a second-generation Mexican American, told me what his sister had said about some exuberant celebration of a Mexican national holiday in the Midwest: "If those Mexicans love Mexico so much, why don't they go back there?" "How quick we are to shed our ethnicity!" I thought. I also recalled conversations with non-Hispanic friends who, having come to experience life on the border between the United States and Mexico, could not understand our seeming lack of solidarity with the poor right across the Rio Grande. One could also point to the number of California Hispanics or Latinos, as some prefer to be called, who voted in favor of Proposition 187, a legislative attempt to severely curtail economic, educational, and health assistance to immigrants.

What is going on here? Is it simply the case of another immigrant group coming into the United States and then pulling in the bridge behind them? I do not think that this explanation, though somewhat true and characteristic of many immigrant groups, is adequate. Ministry among Mexican Americans is not as simple as it might seem to someone who, at first contact with the culture, hears much English spoken and presumes that they are well on their way to being assimilated into the American melting pot. I hope that the seven tips I propose will demonstrate how enigmatic a population this is. The church's response must respect this complexity and demonstrate more sensitivity to God's presence in this culture.

Besides examining some of the literature about Mexican Americans, I consulted several pastoral agents, all of whom are Mexican Americans or Chicanos ministering in this cultural context. At times I render their exact words. Sometimes their comments serve as a catalyst for my own observations. All except one, reside in El Paso, Texas. Two are women religious: Sylvia Chacón, A.S.C., Ann Francis Monedero, O.S.F. Another is a consultant and lay campus minister at the University of La Verne, California: María Elena Cardeña. The

81

fourth is a diocesan priest, pastor of a large, thriving parish in El Paso: Arturo Bañuelas. Chacón's background includes political activism, teaching, writing, giving retreats, working with *comunidades de base* and vocational promotion. Monedero has taught grade school in the deep South, the Midwest, and finally the Southwest, for sixteen years. I recently interviewed each of them individually.

Far from serving as the comprehensive guide to ministry among Mexican Americans, this chapter only reveals the tip of the iceberg. If I can leave the pastoral agent with some serious questions, I feel that I have achieved my goal.

Foster a Positive Cultural Self-identity Among the People

All four of my colleagues demonstrated not only a great amount of self-knowledge in terms of their own identity, but also significant, often torturous journeys to arrive at their present understanding of themselves. In having to leave their hometowns to study or become part of a religious community, they encountered very different customs, diets, norms of behavior. One spoke of later having to confront things about her culture or her family that she found embarrassing; in this case, it was her mother's practices of popular religion. Some noted that their theological training in a United States mainstream environment was sharply challenged when they returned to their native culture. In this way, they spoke of growing to the point where they were again able to embrace their culture.

This search for identity is very apparent in United States Hispanic theology. In a study of a comprehensive bibliography of the writings of Latinas and Latinos during the last twenty-five years, for example, I found that this attempt to name, describe, and embrace who we are, both as individuals and as members of wider communities, ranked highest on the list (Fernández, Eduardo, "Towards a United States Hispanic Theology: A Study of a Current Bibliography," unpublished licentiate thesis. Rome: Pontifical Gregorian University, 1992). Two of the Latinos who shared their own journey in terms of identity and acceptance are Virgilio Elizondo (*The Future Is Mestizo: Life Where Cultures Meet.* Bloomington, IN: Meyer-Stone, 1988) and Roberto Goizueta (*Caminemos con Jesús: Toward a Hispanic/Latino Theology of Accompaniment.* Maryknoll, NY: Orbis Books, 1995).

If identity is an issue for pastoral agents and professional theologians, how much more must it be for Mexican Americans who often do not have the resources to contextualize their situation? Take the example of a family of professionals who happen to be Mexican American. How at-home are they going to feel in a parish whose "Hispanic ministry" is equivalent to "immigrant ministry?" With services often held exclusively in Spanish, with youth groups made up predominantly of the recently arrived, will they have the motivation and linguistic tools to be integrated into this new Hispanic community? Sociologist Andrew Greeley warns us that a significant part of the Hispanic middle and upper class is leaving the church ("Defection Among Hispanics," *America* [30 July, 1988], 61–62). It seems that many middle-class Hispanics no longer feel welcome in a church that is either tailored to "Anglos" (that is, non-Hispanics) or to recently arrived immigrants. I preached a parish mission in New Mexico, where the Hispanic congregation was made of families who had been in that part of the country since 1598, together with those whose grandparents had migrated to the United States from Mexico in the first decade of this century and people who had arrived during the last year—all sitting together in the same pews, all hearing the same exhortations to a life of holiness.

This highlights the dangers of not considering all the varieties found even among Mexican Americans. The search for identity, given the lack of appropriate categories, is in many ways a messy one. My time in New Mexico convinced me that my *mestizo* (mixed/blended) paradigms are not operative in the land of very distinct Pueblo Indian and Spanish cultures.

This lack of universal clarity regarding personal identity should not distract us from the fact that God has blessed us with a specific culture or cultures, and we are who we are by the grace of God. The business of "I will be okay when I become the ideal Mexican American or Chicano who lives in the barrio and is one with the *Raza* (race)" has not been very beneficial to us. Whether we speak Spanish or not, whether our *abuelita* (grandmother) is living in a rancho or running her own corporation, I would argue that there are aspects of who we are that make up what Arturo Bañuelas calls our *mística*, which affirms our cultural identity given all its ambiguities and "provokes our religiosity." How do we become versed in this *mística*? Read on.

Become Versed in Signs and Symbols

Anyone who has ever attended a celebration held on the feast of Our Lady of Guadalupe knows the power her presence evokes in our lives. Various Latino and Latina writers have explored the reasons why our own *Morenita* is so special to us (Elizondo, Virgilio, *La Morenita: Evangelizer of the Americas.* San Antonio: Mexican American Cultural Center, 1980; Rodríguez, Jeanette, *Our Lady of Guadalupe: Faith and Empowerment Among Mexican-American Women.* Austin: University of Texas Press, 1994; and, most recently, a collection of essays by Hispanic writers, published under the controversial title of *Goddess of the Americas/La Diosa de las Americas: Writings on the Virgin of Guadalupe.* New York: Riverhead Books, 1996). A young priest in Las Cruces describes the joy and validation Hispanics in the parish felt when the image of Our Lady of Guadalupe was moved from the vestibule to the sanctuary. It was similar to the experience of African Americans no longer having to sit in the back of the bus.

Theologians Orlando Espín and Arturo Pérez take a more cultural anthropological route to theology, a field which Gustavo Gutierrez calls "God-talk." They are now exploring the role of popular religion in Latino spirituality (Espín, Orlando, *The Faith of the People.* Maryknoll: Orbis, 1997; Pérez, Arturo, *Popular Catholicism.* Washington: Pastoral Press, 1988).

In comparison to United States mainstream culture, Hispanic culture is more comfortable with mystery, a fact which is borne out in the extensive use of symbol and ritual. In the words of Chacón,

> It is like working with a poem, there is something there that you cannot describe. . . . In terms of my people, they are like trees, they are grounded. When they impose hands in blessing, they help me to see.

Mendicant orders carried out much of the early evangelization in Latin America. Franciscans, Dominicans, and Jesuit missionaries did not hesitate to use song, drama, dance, storytelling, visual art, and architecture to present the sacred gospel truths that they were trying to proclaim. Couple that fact with the reality of Native Americans, who already were very tactile in their approach to the Divine, and we have a new blend that is still taking shape as cultures continue to evolve.

In her work with Latino college students, Cardeña found that students responded enthusiastically to such Mexican symbols as Guadalupe, the Chicano eagle, and Emiliano Zapata. She speaks of a profound spirituality among the students whose faith journey can be nourished by biblical imagery such as the eagle reading in Isaiah, or passages speaking of solidarity with one's people. Other prominent symbols, which do not necessarily require use within a eucharistic liturgy, are the distribution of ashes and holy cards. "On a campus, you do not necessarily have to gather people in order to minister to them as they go about their busy day."

Another gold mine for savoring Mexican American symbols and rituals are the murals which are found in many of our barrios (Cockcroft, Eva Sperling, and Holly Barnett-Sánchez, Eds., *Signs from the Heart: California Chicano Murals.* Venice, CA: Social and Public Art Resource Center, 1990). As the New Mexican Santeros knew centuries ago, the image and the stories go hand in hand. Their paintings and sculptures cradle a wealth of religious folk beliefs. In the words of Charlie Carrillo, a contemporary Santero master, "This is one of those art forms you cannot separate from the people. We write our own history by what we say and the art we do" (Awalt, Barbe, and Paul Rhetts, *Charlie Carrillo: Tradition & Soul/Tradición y Alma.* Albuquerque: LPD Press, 1995). In addition, one must not forget that certain symbols are sources of power and empowerment for powerless and disenfranchised communities (Rodríguez, Jeanette, *op. cit.,* and Pulido, Alberto L., "Mexican American Catholicism in the Southwest: the Transformation of a Popular Religion," *Perspectives in Mexican American Studies,* Vol. 4 [1994], 93–108).

Get Educated

Find out as much as you can about Hispanic ministry and the specific Mexican American population you are working with and among. For an idea of the diversity of this population, consider that M. E. Matute-Bianchi identifies five major categories of ethnic identity within the Mexican American student population ("Ethnic Identities and Patterns of School Success and Failure Among Mexican-Descent and Japanese-American Students in a California High School: An Ethnographic Analysis," *American Journal of Education,* Vol. 95 [1986], 233–255). Recent Mexican immigrants may not plan to stay in the country. Some are only here to work for a few months or years.

In fact, according to a recent study, most return home within a few years (*San Francisco Chronicle*, 29 January 1997). Others, though they opt to become citizens of the United States, maintain strong ties to Mexico. Just these two examples illustrate that United States citizens of Mexican descent do not follow the traditional patterns of other European immigrant groups.

A good starter for someone interested in Hispanic ministry, even for someone who has worked in this area for some time but could benefit from a more systematic analysis, is Allan Figueroa Deck's *The Second Wave: Hispanic Ministry and the Evangelization of Cultures* (Mahwah, NJ: Paulist Press, 1989). Deck has also co-edited a valuable collection of essays with Jay P. Dolan entitled *Hispanic Catholic Culture in the United States: Issues and Concerns* (Notre Dame: University of Notre Dame Press, 1994). I also recommend *Mexican Americans and the Catholic Church: 1900–1965* (Dolan, Jay P. and Gilberto M. Hinojosa, eds. Notre Dame: University of Notre Dame Press, 1994). This volume is helpful for acquiring a historical sensitivity toward Mexican Americans in different parts of the country, including the often neglected Midwest. The late Joseph Fitzpatrick offers a tight overview in "A Survey of Literature on Hispanic Ministry" (in *Strangers and Aliens No Longer, Part One: The Hispanic Presence in the Church of the United States*. Washington: NCCB/USCC Office of Research, 1992, 63–92). Kenneth Davis, Verónica Mendez, and I publish an article every spring in the journal, *Review for Religious*, which not only offers resources for Hispanic ministry, but also gives an annotated bibliography of pertinent books and articles that came out the previous year, information about what generally occurred in the Latino communities and what their leaders are doing by way of pastoral work, teaching, and awards.

Pastoral agents would do well to heed the advice which Don C. Locke gives to teachers and therapists working among Mexican Americans: ". . . helping professionals can work to break down any stereotypes they may hold about Mexican Americans by speaking with other professionals who are in contact with Mexican Americans and by reading about the culture of this group" (*Increasing Multicultural Understanding: A Comprehensive Model*. Newbury Park, CA: Sage Publications, 1992).

Keep in mind the need for a thorough social analysis that considers a people's history and the current socioeconomic situation of the specific Mexican American community. Social class probably determines more about a person than ethnicity. One should be suspicious of commonly held assumptions, for instance, that most Hispanics are poor or that they are migrant workers. In fact, according to the 1995 population surveys of the United States Bureau of Labor Statistics, 29.6% of Mexican Americans are below the poverty level. Barring those who are undocumented and therefore often not surveyed, that means that about 70% are not. Almost 32% have household incomes of $35,000 or more. Often not taken into account are recently arrived immigrants who are from the Mexican middle class. Their situation is very different from poor immigrants, and pastoral strategies suitable for those with little or no formal education would not be appropriate.

Contrary to the myth that most Mexican Americans are farm workers, the same bureau's 1995 figures show that only 8.3% are in farming, forestry, and fishing jobs. These statistics mean that we have many urban, middle-class Mexican Americans whom, I believe, want to do something for the less fortunate members of society.

Although one would never guess from the dearth of material available on ministry to Hispanic youth and young adults, a significant portion, 34% of the Mexican American population, is under the age of fourteen (1995 data, United States Bureau of the Census). The sociological consequences of having such a huge population of youths are enormous. As Wade Clark Roof and Christel Manning note, the issues of the role of identity and cultural conflict are very pertinent ones ("Cultural Conflicts and Identity: Second-Generation Hispanic Catholics in the United States," *Social Compass*, Vol. 41(1) [1994], 171–184).

Other socioeconomic studies reveal some interesting trends among Mexican Americans. Consistent with the tendency for immigrant groups in the United States to hold to their Catholicism because it is part of who they are as a national group, Mexican immigrants are less likely to abandon their religion, since it is seen as constitutive of their ethnicity. It is true that while three-quarters of persons of Mexican origin say they are Catholic, almost one-half say they never or almost never attend religious services (De la Garza, Rodolfo O., Louis De Sipio, F. Chris Garcia, John Garcia, and Angelo Falcon, *Latino Voices: Mexican, Puerto Rican, and Cuban Perspectives on American Politics*. Boulder: Westview, 1992). However, church attendance is not the only criterion for measuring religiosity. Already I have spoken of the prevalence of popular religion. Similarly, in this study, 63% of persons of Mexican origin said that they receive a great deal or quite a bit of guidance from religion. I am reminded of what John Fitzpatrick, then bishop of the diocese of Brownsville, told us novices back in the early 1980s about the poor Hispanics living in his diocese:

> They may not attend church every Sunday, nor be married by the Church, nor receive the sacraments regularly, but they are among the most Christian persons I have ever met. They help each other out with whatever they can and pull together in times of difficulties.

Don't Ignore the Role of Families and Friends

The relational component in Hispanic culture cannot be over-stressed. In many ways, the ideal is not how much money you acquire, but how many friends you have. The appeal among Latino young people of the song "Quiero tener un millión de amigos" ("I want to have a million friends") never ceases to amaze me. The same can be said for the warmth and support of family. While United States mainstream culture tends to be task-oriented, Hispanic culture is person-oriented. Therefore, as Bañuelas reminded me, "family" means much more than the nuclear family. Grandparents, aunts, uncles, and cousins are all part of that special community that nourishes and educates, but also makes demands.

A practical consequence of this focus on relationships means that human contact is very important. Face-to-face transactions are much preferred to those conducted over telephone lines. Courtesy demands civilities before doing business. A simple "buenos días," as our parishioners reminded me, is extremely important. The elders are afforded great respect. And many of us were taught never to use the familiar verb form in Spanish with them. These older members of the family or of the community, notwithstanding their economic status, have earned such noble titles as "don" and "doña." The godparents of a child enter into a relationship not only with the child but also with her or his parents. They become "compadres" (co-parents).

An understanding of the importance of relationality for Hispanics in general can provide cues for tapping into communal values already present. As medical sociologist David Hayes-Bautista once told me:

> If you want someone from United States mainstream culture to stop smoking, you tell them that it is bad for *their* health. On the other hand, if you want a Hispanic to do the same, you tell them to think about what it will be like for *their children* if they die of cancer.

Cardeña provided another example of how familial values can serve as a bridge to educational advancement, especially important for a population whose college graduation rate is only 6.5%. A young woman who is not being allowed to leave home to study might remind her parents of the importance of "la prosperidad de la familia," which would include taking care of them when they are older. Another practical strategy suggested by Cardeña is having these parents speak to others whose daughters have left home. While it should be acknowledged that the daughter will change, that does not mean that she will stop respecting them. Rosa María Gil and Carmen Inoa Vázquez propose a similar road of openness and dialogue in their recent book *The María Paradox: How Latinas Can Merge Old World Traditions with New World Self-Esteem* (New York: G.P. Putnam's Sons, 1996). The campus minister also reminds us of our need to ritualize these young people's going away to school. Give them a blessing, acknowledge them in church.

Those who leave the Hispanic community for religious vocations or marriage bring with them certain understandings or expectations of what family should be about. It is difficult when they are not met. One woman religious I interviewed said that her community was supposed to be a family, but that it did not feel like one. For example, since she was supposedly being formed to be at the service of the community, one would imagine that relationality, belonging, was important. Yet, close relationships among the sisters, or "particular friendships," in the phrase of many religious communities, were discouraged.

While there is often much strength in Mexican American familial bonds, we have to be careful not to romanticize. There may be a price which a particular member, most often the mother, must pay. At times the desires and gifts of the individual are sacrificed to the larger unit. As Cardeña said about students who may want to pursue the fine arts, "It is difficult to be creative when you are from a family of *obreros* (workers)."

Machismo is also said to be a problem, about which Cardeña offers insight. At times, a husband will use the "it's always been that way" rationalization to justify oppression of his wife. The concept of cultural stagnation, however, reminds us that if we do not adapt to our current world and let go of what is supposedly the "Mexican way" (as if nothing has changed in industrialized Mexico in the last fifty years), we will find ourselves following "outdated road maps."

I have neither the expertise nor the space to begin to discuss such difficult familial topics as domestic violence, sexual abuse, and other dysfunctions which may come up in counseling or confessional situations. Consider, for example, what happens when young people migrate from Mexico and find themselves in close living arrangements. As with sexual abuse involving clergy or a family member, it is very difficult even to begin to speak about these things. I leave that topic to more qualified persons. However, I think we, as pastoral agents, must be very sensitive in these trying family matters. At least we must be able to refer those who, as a result of these patterns, need professional help.

Meet People on Their Own Turf

As Monedero stated, "Enter into this culture with the understanding that God is already present and that, therefore, there is much I can discover about who God is through this culture, this land, these people." This open attitude of acknowledging that we pastoral agents are not only the proponents of ministry, but also the recipients of it, will prompt me to visit people in their homes, on their campuses, at their place of employment. At all times, we suspend judgment about their ways and always keep in mind that there is much more going on than meets the eye.

A good example of Monedero's advice is studying the custom of the *quinceañera* as a rite of passage. The people may not explain it in those terms, but they know in their heart that this ritual of thanking, blessing, and sending forth is important for young women. Chacón summarized the parents' financial sacrifice to make it special: "*Aunque nos cueste, es algo que le podemos aportar*" (Even though it may cost us, it is something we can bestow).

I was recently reminded of modern Western culture's lack of

appropriate rituals when I heard a professor in California say, "I have to invent some appropriate rites of passage for my son." One does not normally invent rites of passage. A nurturing society should be able to provide them. If there is anything that sociology has taught us it is that we do not invent ourselves. As the mother of a priest, pointing to her son's Roman collar and then to the ring on her finger, said to him on his ordination day, "You would not have that if it weren't for this!"

Returning to the importance of *personalismo*, or this relational component in ministry, I cite the words of the great priest sociologist and pioneer in Hispanic ministry, Joseph Fitzpatrick, S.J., "The major failure in Hispanic ministry is not to have developed a personalistic ministry, in small-group settings and in a style with which Hispanics feel at home" (*op cit.*).

An insightful remark made at a recent presbyterial celebration in a west Texas mission town was that the lay people were invited to participate by contributing their talents, that is, because of their cultural richness. So whether they sang, played, danced, cleaned, cooked, decorated, proclaimed the Word, or just looked pretty, they were all contributing to the fiesta atmosphere where the line between the sacred and the profane become blurred. The mother of the young man who was ordained remarked, "*El baile era porque la gente estaba muy contenta que se recibió un padre*" (The community danced because they rejoiced that they had a new priest.)

This meeting of Mexican Americans on their turf does not mean absolutizing their culture. Inculturation is about identifying and incarnating gospel values, not about absolutizing any one culture. All cultures are in need of conversion. I asked Bañuelas how he spoke of conversion to his Hispanic middle-class parishioners, especially since his community is considered cutting-edge in the diocese. His response is very revealing.

> They don't feel at home with the option for the poor. They feel that they have worked hard to get where they are, and even though they are willing to help the others come up, they do not necessarily agree that they are responsible for the poverty of these people.

This Mexican American pastor contrasts the message that this Hispanic middleclass is hearing from some Protestant churches, "health and wealth," with what we appear to be saying: "You're to blame for the poverty in the world."

"How then do you move them beyond that lack of conformity to the social gospel?" I asked. "Since your parish has a significant outreach, how did you accompany them to that point?" His answer was concise:

> I pushed solidarity. Once they got to know the poor personally or the victims of AIDS, for example, they had to deal with the unhappiness in their own lives. They fear that they've lost the soul! It is during these times that they realize that the message of "health and wealth" is anti-Catholic.

Be Authentic. Know Your Own Story and Celebrate It

Just as Mexican Americans grapple with their identity, so do other inhabitants of the United States. This grappling, however, is not always so obvious when you belong to the dominant culture. I wonder sometimes if there is not hidden, deep in an ethnic group's collective consciousness, much pain involving assimilation which has never been addressed. I am thinking of a woman of Italian descent who was too embarrassed to tell me her maiden name. Greer Gordon, the African American theologian who teaches at Regis College in Weston, Massachusetts, feels that much of the racial antipathy on our campuses is the product of children of immigrants who had to hide who they were. In a campus ministry workshop, she reminded us that it was not long ago that Irish people were not allowed into certain places in Boston. Unfortunately, these stories often get lost. My cousin, for example, was never told that our grandfather was a *bracero*, a contracted farm worker from Mexico.

Chacón recommends that we get in touch with our own pain of assimilation. Her experience in Wichita, Kansas, taught her that people often try to cut themselves off from where they came. "Ours is an absolutist culture which stifles diversity . . . we, as ministers, are in a position to remind people that they, too, were once strangers in a foreign land." According to her, if we want to immerse ourselves in a culture, we need to tell our own stories. If we share how we came to tap into our own sense of the sacred, others will reflect on their own journey.

Dare to be Messy, Chaotic, Creative and Human

Bernard Lonergan, S.J., described conversion as the broadening of one's horizons. In the area of multicultural ministry, an authentic encounter with the riches of a specific culture reveals the face of a God whom we might not have experienced otherwise in quite the same way. For example, as one of my liturgy professors, James Empereur, S.J., used to remind us, "Liturgy can be messy, but messy does not mean meaningless." I have heard him say that, while he used to preach against cluttered sanctuaries, now that he is working in a Hispanic context, he is finding that he has experienced some of the best liturgies in cluttered sanctuaries.

Anthropologists constantly remind us that there is always much more going on in a human context than meets the eye. As any good teacher knows, quiet in a classroom does not necessarily mean that learning is taking place. The intangibility of much of what goes on in good liturgy, especially in the best aesthetic sense, is a gateway to the sacred. And this sense of the sacred does not always take place within church walls. Chacón credits the graceful dance of El Paso's educator and culturalist Rosa Guerrero as a catalyst for her "conversion." Steeped largely in the anger of her political activism, she was introduced to another way of working toward multi-cultural unity and divine harmony: Creating beauty! It comes as no surprise that a culture known for its artistic ability can celebrate vivacious liturgies.

As these seven "tips" have demonstrated, the most important qualities needed for work with and among Mexican Americans are the very same ones that grace any human encounter. I close with a quote I remember hearing from the African American writer Maya Angelou, one attributed to a black slave living in the time of ancient Rome: "Nothing which is human is foreign to me." May this human encounter between different racial and ethnic groups in the heart of the church be a living sign of that mystical body of Christ alive in the world today.

HISPANIC CATHOLIC YOUTH IN THE UNITED STATES

George Boran, C.S.S.P.

A national congress for Hispanic ministry called "Roots and Wings," held at Loyola University, Chicago, in August 1996 opened new possibilities for the organization of Hispanic Catholics in the United States. The congress was attended by nearly 900 delegates from 41 states, including 18 bishops. Selected people involved in Hispanic youth ministry were invited to participate in a special youth track. I was fortunate to be part of this group. At the end of the Congress, a committee was elected to put together the building blocks of a national organization for Hispanic Catholic youth.

The Context and the Challenge

According to Alan Figueroa Deck, S.J., then executive director of the National Catholic Council for Hispanic Ministry (NCCHM), the organization that promoted the Chicago Congress, "Hispanics are now 30% of American Catholics (about 24 million). By the turn of the century, they will be the majority. They already are in California, Florida and Texas." The number of Hispanic Catholics has increased five times faster than the number of Euro-American Catholics.

While there is still considerable prejudice against the Hispanic population in the wider society and even within the Catholic Church, Hispanics have come together and built strong organizations on both national and local levels to voice their pastoral needs.

Without doubt, young people are one of the most important and difficult challenges for Hispanic ministry. Hispanics are the ethnic group with the youngest median age in the United States. Their average age is 23.2; 54% are age 25 or under; yet it is estimated that 95% have no link with the institutional church. It is a challenge that cannot be ignored. An unwelcoming attitude toward Hispanic youth pushes many of them into Pentecostal sects or the surrounding culture's whirlpool of materialism and secularism. An answer to this challenge cannot be put off. A church that is unable to count on the presence and dynamism of young people faces a serious threat to its own survival.

The following reflections offer some ideas on how this challenge can be met through a ministry specifically for Hispanic youth. I bring to the writing of this article both disadvantages and advantages. The principal disadvantage is the limited time I have worked with Hispanic youth ministry in the United States—only three and a half years. However, I have the advantage of having worked for almost 30 years on Latin American and Brazilian coordination committees of youth ministry, and thus am in touch with the cultural roots of American Hispanics. My Irish-American background is helpful in understanding a First World context. In my dissertation, completed in 1996 at Fordham University, I studied and contrasted both the American and the Latin American models of youth ministry. As an "outsider," I believe I can bring to this discussion perspectives that are not otherwise readily available. There is always the danger of not seeing the forest for the trees.

The Right to Be Different

Hispanic youth ministry is organized not only to meet the language difficulties of some Hispanics, but also because the process of evangelization needs to be incarnated in the culture of each human group. John Paul II points out that when faith meets culture three things happen: The culture is purified, the best of that culture is enhanced, and the church itself is enriched.

The relationship of Hispanics with other cultures can be considered from two different perspectives. On one hand, it is important for Hispanic youth to mix with young people of other cultures, especially the mainstream culture. This is the nature of the church: Persons relate to one another as brothers and sisters in the same faith.

On the other hand, this goal can be better achieved when differences are accepted and Hispanic youth have an opportunity to establish their own identity, cultivating their cultural and linguistic origins. The Special Subtask Panel of American Hispanics (1979) points out, "The Hispanic youths have been forced to experience emotional disorientation, feelings of inferiority and very low self-image and self-esteem." The typical problems of adolescents are aggravated by discrimination in some parishes. Many Hispanic youth have the feeling of being outsiders in their own church. In their document, *Brothers and Sisters to Us* (1979), the bishops acknowledge the need to face the sin of racism within the church itself, "a sin that divides the human family, blots out the image of God among specific members of that family and violates the fundamental human dignity of those called to be children of the same Father."

Many young Hispanics also suffer racial and economic discrimination in the wider society. This seriously harms young people, especially during adolescence when they are in the process of discovering their own personality, improving their self-image, and establishing an autonomous identity. By valuing their cultural roots and combating images from the dominant culture that they are powerless and stupid, young Hispanics gain a new control over their lives. This new-found dignity is possible only to the extent that they are not ashamed of their cultural origins. It is only then, when young people have reached a certain confidence in themselves and an appreciation of their own cultural and religious expressions, that they are capable of meeting the religious expressions of other cultures in a mature way.

In the 1980 document, *Beyond the Melting Pot: Cultural Pluralism in the United States*, the American bishops laid to rest the theory that the melting pot would eliminate all cultural and racial differences. More apt images, such as a salad or a rainbow, are used. The message of the early church has not been forgotten. The first Council of Jerusalem was called to discuss the need to acculturate the gospel in the new context of non-Jews. One Hispanic church leader points out: "We must always keep in mind that the church's task is evangelization, not 'Americanization.'" Many ethnic groups of earlier times, such as the Irish, the Italians, and the Poles, integrated into the American mainstream without giving up their own deeply rooted cultural values. A bumper sticker I saw in New York summed up a happy marriage. Underneath an Italian flag was written: "My heritage." Underneath an American flag was written: "My country." The challenge today is to remind those Catholics who have made it up the economic ladder that solidarity with today's "huddled masses"—among whom are many Hispanic Catholics—should be a consequence of loyalty to the struggle of their own ancestors.

Hispanic youth groups and the wider Hispanic youth ministry are important spaces where young Hispanics can learn to face the challenge of living in two cultures (in the wider society and at home) and can contend with the specific obstacles that prevent the gospel from becoming an effective force in their lives. This means working with

English and Spanish, a decided advantage in a new world order where globalization is a central trend. The fact that the United States today ranks fifth in population among the world's Spanish-speaking countries should not be a cause for concern, as it is in some circles. The ability to speak more than one language is an increasing necessity.

Some pastors fear that the organization of a separate ministry for Hispanic youth could harm the unity of the parish community. This is a legitimate concern. A specific youth ministry must not be an excuse for not offering Hispanic youth the skills for cross-cultural communication with people from the dominant culture. The solution is not to deny Hispanic youths the right to organize, but rather to plan activities and moments in which both the Spanish-speaking and the English-speaking youth ministries can come together to exchange ideas and experiences and build unity. In the diocese where I worked, representatives from both youth ministries met regularly to exchange ideas and experiences and to plan activities together. The act of coming together and talking about what we have in common and what makes us different is a fundamental step forward. Martin Luther King, Jr., indicated an important motive for such contact: "Racism is caused by fear, and fear is caused by separation."

However, integration must not be confused with assimilation. Integration implies a process of accepting both one's own group and the other group. Young people are especially positioned to be natural bridges between both the Hispanic and Euro-American cultures. They are the social group most open to discovering the common humanity and the common faith that unite us all. As a response to the first Synod of Bishops of the Americas, such bridge-building becomes more important.

Two Further Conclusions

For my dissertation, I interviewed successful youth ministers in the United States and in Latin American countries. The United States ministers were from English-speaking youth ministries. Since the American participants in this qualitative study came from only three dioceses in the northeastern part of the country, I do not wish to generalize the conclusions to a national population. The findings, nevertheless, do present real models, and have a bearing on pastoral options the emergent national Hispanic organization for youth must consider. A temptation for Hispanics may be to seek inspiration only in the Euro-American models of youth ministry without also examining important Latin American perspectives that may be better adapted to the cultural background of Hispanic young people.

I will examine two of the more important conclusions, namely, the contrast between psychological and sociological models, and the tension between two very different organizational approaches to youth ministry.

Psychological and Sociological Models

The United States participants emphasize a psychological model in which relationships are central. Latin American participants, on the other hand, give priority to a sociological model in which social analysis is the focus. A deeper understanding of both models is important if Hispanic youth ministry is to make the correct choice.

The youth minister involved in the psychological model sees his or her role as giving priority to the psychological forces at work in the young person's life, and presenting the gospel message as an answer to the psychological challenges faced by the young person. Central to the psychological model is the question of relationships. But there are limitations. While this model offers valuable insights for dealing with the psychological problems young people face, it is ill equipped for dealing with surrounding social problems. The solutions for poverty and discrimination—when they are considered—follow a line of alleviating symptoms rather than causes.

Latin American participants believe that the main role of the adult minister is to help young people acquire the critical skills for analyzing the structural causes of poverty and marginalization of minority groups in society. The building of a more just and fraternal society is possible only to the extent that people discover and eliminate the structural causes of poverty. Personal conversion is also fundamental, but cannot be divorced from structural change.

This focus is difficult for youth ministry. Structures are invisible. Although they exercise enormous influence on the quality of life and human values, people are largely unaware of them. A Vatican document, *Instruction on Christian Freedom and Liberation* (1986), highlights the importance of these structures: "Being necessary in themselves, they often tend to become fixed and fossilized as mechanisms relatively independent of the human will, thereby paralyzing or distorting social development and causing injustice."

The emphasis of the Latin American participants is partly influenced by a different social and church context: the extremes of poverty and riches in the southern countries, and the development of a theology which uses the tools of the social sciences to analyze the social situation to be evangelized. The concern for social justice is a legitimate objective for a Latin American youth ministry, but is also relevant to the United States context.

The literature supports the inclusion of the sociological model as an essential aspect of youth ministry in both continents. Nationally known leaders such as Tom Zanzig call attention to the need to:

> actively engage young people in action on behalf of social justice, awakening within them a consciousness of how they are manipulated by the media and other dimensions of our culture and then providing the guidance they need to combat these negative influences in their lives. (*The Journal of Youth Ministry*, Winter 1983)

No one can deny our Christian responsibilities in these areas. The document *Justice in the World* (Synod of Bishops, 1972) points out that the work for justice is a "constitutive dimension of the preaching of the Gospel" (6). The United States bishops analyze a reality that the youth minister must consider in work with young people.

> Poverty is increasing in the United States, not decreasing. For a people who believe in "progress," this should be cause for alarm. These burdens fall most heavily on blacks, Hispanics, and Native Americans. Even more disturbing is the large increase in the number of women and children living in poverty. Today children are the largest single group among the poor. This tragic fact seriously threatens the nation's future. That so many people are poor in a nation as rich as ours is a social and moral scandal that we cannot ignore. (*Economic Justice for All*, 1986)

In the United States, both youth ministers and youth are exposed to a constant barrage of ideas provoked by political debate on the national budget, interest groups, education, environment, health care, housing, employment, minimum wage, welfare, and violence. These are themes that touch on the lives of everyone and are frequent in the media and ordinary conversations. Without an understanding of structural causes and interest groups, young people are reduced to passivity regarding the great questions of our time. They are easily manipulated by 30-second sound bites that offer simplistic solutions and ignore the complexity of issues. Hispanic and black youth are the two social groups that most acutely suffer the consequences of these unjust structures in American society. For Hispanics to overcome a deep inferiority complex caused by their marginalization in society, some sort of understanding of the surrounding social structures of which they are victims is necessary. Not all the blame for their inferior status can be placed on them or their parents.

The findings, therefore, reveal that the United States participants give primacy to relationships (psychological model) and the Latin American participants give primacy to the promotion of social justice (sociological model). These are the conclusions drawn from the people interviewed. In reality, however, there is no clear distinction. In some parts of the United States the sociological model is also used, and in some parts of Latin America the psychological model is the only focus.

An emergent Hispanic youth ministry should not fall into the trap of an either/or choice between the psychological and sociological models. A mature youth ministry in either continent will use the tools of both psychology and sociology to present the gospel message and maintain a balance between the individual and the social. Youth leaders accept more readily a youth ministry that gives priority to relationships. Social justice seems irrelevant in the modern world. The consequence of this option is the formation of young people who are naive and alienated, followers not leaders. On the other hand, a youth ministry that gives priority to social justice—to the exclusion of relationships—simply does not work. Young people are not motivated and do not become involved. In the past, overemphasis in Latin America on the sociological dimension to the exclusion of the psychological has frequently led to a largely ineffective Hispanic youth ministry. Pastoral work with Hispanic young people needs to avoid getting locked into an either/or choice.

The psychological model (micro level of personal relationships) and the sociological model (macro level of relations in the wider society) are interconnected. The young person is linked to both the micro and macro levels, and a balanced youth ministry should help the young person to grow and contribute on both planes. Hispanic youth are called to live out the consequences of their faith commitment in both contexts.

Synthesis: Latin American Model of Stages

The stages of education in the faith, as defined by the Latin American youth ministry, are a useful instrument for integrating both the psychological and the sociological models. In the initial stages (discovery of the group, of the church community, of the surrounding social problems, and of the wider youth organization) preference is given to the psychological model. In the latter stages (discovery of the structural causes of social problems, of commitment, and of an awareness of the previous pedagogical stages), the sociological model receives more attention.

A detailed explanation of these stages is in my book, *Youth Ministry That Works* (Mahwah, NJ: Paulist Press, 1996). In practice, youth leaders must start with the psychological model to be effective in motivating and involving young people. But young people should also be challenged to move beyond a therapeutic pattern in pastoral ministry, with its emphasis on building self-esteem and solving individual problems, to an awareness of responsibility for the wider human family, especially disadvantaged groups. An effective ministry to Hispanic youth should prepare them for involvement in public life as a consequence of their faith and duty as citizens. In *Revolution From Within* (Boston: Little, Brown, 1993), Gloria Steinem has summed up the challenge: "It's as if the two great movements of our time, those for social justice and for self-realization, were halves of a whole just waiting to come together into truly revolutionary groups."

Two Different Models of Organization

A second conclusion from the United States/Latin American study has to do with different organizational models. The United States group understood this organization as a diocesan office that offers services to young people in parishes. The Latin American group understood youth ministry as a network of parish youth groups, knit together by means of coordination teams on different levels.

Participants from the United States dioceses at the "Roots and Wings" congress noted the lack of an effective networking system, even at the level of adult youth ministers. They lamented the isolation of youth groups. The diocesan youth offices worked very much as a top-down service.

Latin American participants take the networking approach a step further. They have a clear vision of the need for a networking system not only among adult youth ministers but also among the young people themselves. Pastoral planning, evaluation, and youth coordination teams are important ingredients. Coordination committees are organized on different levels: national, regional, diocesan, parochial.

Distinct terminology illustrates the differences. While the United States participants talk of a "diocesan office" of youth ministry, their Latin American counterparts talk about the "diocesan youth coordination." The United States youth ministers talk about expectations of organizing "youth programs." Their southern neighbors prefer to speak of launching "processes of formation." When the United States participants talk about the need for supporting structures, they usually refer to bureaucratic structures, files, computers, a well-equipped office. When the Latin American participants talk about the need for structures, they are more concerned with organizational arrangements such as coordination committees, evaluation and planning assemblies that are a guarantee that youth are a part of the decision-making process. This is the organizational model which gives young people a sense of ownership of their own ministry. Promoting youth as protagonists or principal actors of their own educational development avoids exclusive control by adults.

The role of the adult youth minister in each model is obviously very different. In the first, the adults make most of the decisions and do most of the coordinating and organization. Youth are very often passive receivers. In the second, the adult minister is more of a guide, a mentor, a coach, a spiritual director. The adult assumes more of a background role, seeking to place young people on center stage. However, some balance between the two extremes is necessary. One Anglo youth minister summed up the challenge:

> In the past, in order to empower young people, we handed everything over to them. The result was chaos. We then went to the other extreme and centralized everything in the hands of the adults. We need to work toward a partnership between adults and young people in which youth are

empowered but not in such a way that they are left to fend for themselves.

The National Federation for Catholic Youth Ministry (NFCYM) is aware of the challenge and has already set up a committee to examine ways of empowering young people.

As Hispanic youth ministry takes its first steps in building its own national organization, it will be obliged to opt between these models. The temptation to adopt a "top-down-only" or "adult-only" run organization is very real. In my judgment, the consequences are disastrous for the motivation of young people, the formation of leadership, and the promotion of the young as the principal evangelizers of their fellow youth.

Power and Leadership

The key issue addressed by the "Roots and Wings" congress was leadership. There is a need to choose a model of leadership that sees power as service rather than self-promotion and domination. This is the gospel model. A complaint that I have heard continually from Hispanics is the presence of centralizing leaders, "caudillos," who see emerging new leaders as dangerous competitors.

Organizational structures can be built so that they promote team work, internal democracy, ownership, leadership, and a community model of church. On the other hand, they can be shaped as a pyramid model of church which reinforces authoritarian behavior and attitudes.

During my stay in the United States, I served as adviser to the Hispanic youth of Rockville Centre diocese on Long Island and had an opportunity to experiment with a more process-oriented, network-structured organization of youth ministry that sought to empower young people. A coordination team that was never able to mobilize more than 15 young people for diocesan events witnessed a transformation; after only a year and a half of working with the new methodology a fresh central committee took on the youth ministry with an impressive degree of dedication and responsibility. A larger diocesan council, composed of representatives of parish groups, was formed. A centralizing leadership was replaced by a leadership that insisted on delegating and distributing responsibilities; a new spirit of enthusiasm and ownership developed among members. As the youth ministry grew, new leaders emerged and new parish groups were integrated into the network. Diocesan events drew large numbers of young people. Motivation grew to the extent that young people felt they were part of the decision-making process.

My experience with Hispanic youth in the United States left me with a strong conviction: it was surprisingly easy to get young people involved and to take on leadership roles. Hispanic youth have a strong need for friendship, community, involvement, to have their talents recognized, and to discover a deeper spiritual meaning for their lives. These are needs to which very often only a church ministry can respond. Perhaps due to the situation of marginalization in which many Hispanics find themselves, the harvest is ripe. Later it may be too late. However, harvesters are needed who can relate the gospel to the cultural context of Hispanics, thus helping young people to be proud of their heritage as an essential ingredient in establishing a healthy self-esteem. There is a need for harvesters who can present this message as a response to the psychological needs of young Hispanics while preparing them as agents of change in their surrounding environment. Harvesters are also needed who understand that when organizational structures promote young people as the principal agents of their own formation, they release enormous energy through which youth become the privileged evangelizers of other young people.

STILL GRINGO
AFTER ALL THESE YEARS:
THE MINISTER IN A
CROSS-CULTURAL CONTEXT

Kenneth G. Davis, O.F.M., Conv.

Introduction

I am admittedly an amateur, that is, one motivated by *amor*, a passion for the oldest, fastest-growing, and soon to be the largest ethnic group of Christians in this country: the United States Hispanic community. Those of us who are not Latino/a have much to learn from them. If privileged to minister in their context, we must understand and adapt our ministry to their worldview.

However, there is little appropriate preparation offered in seminaries, no professional organizations for cross-cultural pastors, and sparse literature on non-Latinos and non-Latinas who minister to Christian churches increasingly Hispanic. We are often cultural amphibians: never insiders to the communities we serve and, by our avocation, always on the margins of the culture from which we come.

On the cusp of ecclesial life, we have personal struggles to overcome, a public role to negotiate, much to learn from Hispanics, and much to share and compare among ourselves. Thus, I divide this chapter into four sections: (1) my personal journey into cultural differences; (2) reflections on the public role of the cross-cultural pastor; (3) the *luminarias* I have encountered on this path; and (4) some practical pointers gleaned from this life's labor. Far from the last word, it is probably the first! And like any cross-cultural ministry, it is a work in process.

My Personal Journey into Cultural Differences

As a missionary in Honduras, I adapted fairly quickly to the lack of potable water, electricity, and familiar food. The reason was that I had some control over those situations. I could boil the water, plug in batteries, and bus to the capital for my Dunkin' Donuts. What I could not control and, therefore found much more unsettling, was the lack of privacy, the accepted intermingling of personal with professional activities, and the hissing.

Yes, hissing! I hiss at a strange cat I want to drive off. Hondurans, however, hiss to attract another person's attention. When they hiss at me, I therefore feel feline. Even more frustrating were appointments with my lawyer which would be continually interrupted by visits from his carpenter, in-laws, and vendors of every description.

What I consider disrespectful of professional boundaries, personal space, and good manners (e.g., a hiss) must be continually reassessed if my ministry among Latino/as is to be effective. And, of course, I must also remember that Hispanics, without an insider's knowledge, may think my own culture odd.

I once cajoled a private school in Chicago into recruiting more Hispanic students. While I could not convince them to hire Hispanic teachers or put more money into scholarships, I did convince the principal to meet with interested parents. After hours of visiting homes and distributing brochures, I finally gathered a few hundred local Latino/as to meet her. She walked in wearing jeans, no jewelry or makeup, and spent much of the meeting seated with her feet propped on a desk. I tried to convince myself that the meeting was going well, but my intuition made my stomach churn as from hot chiles. And, in fact, the recruitment was disastrous.

For many Anglos, such as the principal and me, her appearance and carriage expressed convivial informality. But, for our audience, it connoted rudeness. Just as I can misunderstand Latino/as parishioners, they can find me unintelligible as a pastor.

Reflections on the Public Role of the Pastor in Cross-Cultural Ministry

While I must always monitor my personal journey when ministering to people who are not of my own culture, I need also attend to the public aspect of my ministry as well. There is, of course, a connection between the two since the pastor is one person. Below are reflections on that nexus always at the center of the privilege and the pathos of this endeavor.

A basic assumption is that the pastor is the person who must wrestle with this issue in the context of his or her ministry. Parishioners may or may not have to deal with language problems, prejudice, or cultural misunderstandings outside the church setting.

However, they should *not* have to do so in a ministerial relationship with their pastor.

The responsibility to adapt is the pastor's. He is the person called to ministry; he is the person who answered that call; and he is the person accountable to the community for whom he was called.

If pastoring entails communication, then it must involve the whole person. Therefore, culture and personal experience are of paramount importance. The way a particular Latino/a community interprets the world and processes information may be very different from the minister's. When a pastor is unaware of these differences, places no importance on them, or refuses to adapt to them, miscommunication is inevitable.

A pastor must deal with personal issues which cause these conflicts in such a way that they do not spill into the public ministry. For the cross-cultural minister to do this, he must first make explicit to himself those implicit attitudes and values which inform that ministry and which are not be shared by his parishioners. Next, the pastor must critically reflect on those values and attitudes: Which are based solely on class or cultural idiosyncrasies? Which are truly Gospel based?

A good source for the criteria needed to make this reflection is Manuel Ortiz's *One New People: Models for Developing a Multiethnic Church* (Downers Grove, IL: Intervarsity Press, 1996). It includes a helpful definition of "multiculturalism":

> The end or goal of multiculturalism should not be increased cultural sensitivity or inclusivism so that no one is locked outside the gate (although that is extremely important). Rather, it should be to see the church, by way of multi-ethnicity, inclusivism and cultural sensitivity, bring about biblical reconciliation, justice and righteousness in church and in society.

As Ortiz explains, without this goal and the means to it, the pastor is a captive of culture unable either to critique prophetically her or his own country and class or to preach a liberating word to persons of different socioeconomic and cultural backgrounds.

It is precisely a reflective experience with persons different than oneself that gives a pastor the perspective needed to do this self-critique. Theologian Arturo Bañuelas explained this self-critique: "The task of theology today is not to answer the question: 'Who is God?' Rather the question today is: 'Whose God?'"

When one finally encounters God in a foreign face, the cross of cultural clash becomes a tree bearing new life. Perhaps the greatest blessing of learning Spanish and working with Latina/os is simply the liberating realization that the horizon of human experience, and thus God's revelation, is not encompassed by cultural icons such as Billy Graham and Fulton Sheen. It also includes César Chávez and Dolores Huerta. Only through an empathetic encounter with the other can one really begin to know oneself and one's culture of origin. Just as someone cannot see the candles which light the path to church on Christmas (i.e., *luminarias*) unless the church is dark, so no one can appreciate the "Godlight" from other cultures without consciously dimming the brightness of one's own society.

Luminarias I Have Encountered on This Path

When illuminated by the Gospel, every cultural group has its shadows. This is often obvious to someone of another country. However, the opposite is also true. Respectful dialogue with a different culture provides the pastor a perspective from which to better critique the darkness within his or her own culture. Just as one cannot see the distant stars when surrounded by too much electric light, so the reflective personal journey and public ministry provide the needed contrast to appreciate other *luminarias*.

Based on my own cross-cultural experience and research, I would like to give attention to the *luminarias* which have lighted my path: (1) the value of the discounted; (2) the rejection of the tyranny of technology; (3) the acceptance of destiny; and (4) the ecstasy of aesthetics.

1. The value of the discounted

At a meeting of Hispanic leaders in California, I suggested a procession as a closing prayer. The younger Hispanics thought the idea much too old-fashioned. However, their elders reminded them that pilgrimages, home altars, etc., were precisely what had kept the Faith alive when clergy were scarce and liturgists nonexistent. Why not allow the domestic church, youth and children, women and the elder-

ly or the theologically unsophisticated, to take leadership by celebrating these symbols of the Faith?

Virgil Elizondo and others see the United States Hispanic com-
munity as sociologically singular because they are twice discounted.
Dominant society in this country relegates them to the margins.
Those South of the border often also consider them culturally impure.

Elizondo's *Galilean Journey: The Mexican American Promise*
(Maryknoll, NY: Orbis Books, 1983) posits that Jesus was also twice
rejected. The Jewish community of Jerusalem thought him a Galilean
peasant. The conquering Romans found him threatening. Like the
United States Hispanic, Jesus was rejected by his own and by the
conqueror. Double rejection leading to divine election has become
commonplace in both Protestant and Catholic Hispanic theology.
Like a good shopper, God sees the value of the discounted.

2. The rejection of the tyranny of technology

I accept the tyranny of the clock (even the demands of E-mail)
and am frustrated when a wedding or other ceremony is delayed. But
more than one Cursillista or Charismatic has asked me: "What is more
important for worship: That the community is ready or that the clock
is?"

I realize that respect for another person's time is important. But
are there not moments when a pastor can conform to the timeline of
the community, especially a community which may have to work
long hours, deal with lengthy commutes, and crumbling mass transit?

Moreover, time is a theological concept. As Christians we believe
we live in a time continuum which leads to eternity. Is it not less than
Christian always to think that something precious is lost or robbed by
tardiness? Where your clock is, there your heart will be.

3. The acceptance of destiny

Hispanics are often accused of fatalism when they actually believe
in destiny. If one appreciates harmonious relations with nature rather
than its technological conquest, accepts that there are certain universal
principles that the human cannot or dare not compromise, and
concedes human frailty and fragility, is one a fatalist or a realist? Is
there any aspect of life which must be endured because it cannot be
changed? Is there value to that endurance?

If my culture is particularly good at implementing the second petition of the Serenity prayer, perhaps Latino/as are particularly good at the first.

4. The ecstasy of aesthetics

One semester I helped a student with "Introduction to Philosophy." It presents principles of logic such as: "A statement cannot be both true and false." With all due respect to the handmaid of theology, does this admit the value of paradox?

Many Christian first principles appear self-contradictory (e.g., Jesus is both God and human). I raise this question precisely because I have come to know *mestizos*, i.e., people who are not of pure blood (e.g., Spanish and Native American) but are a biological and cultural mix, a living paradox in a world of racial first principles.

Living this sometimes clashing, seemingly hybrid (e.g., common indigenous, African and Iberian roots), sometimes syncretistic reality leads to an exuberant acceptance of ambiguity, and an almost congenital desire to be inclusive. Witness the baroque and even rococo nature of much Hispanic art.

Severe simplicity and austere orderliness reflect what Justo González calls dominant society's naive reading of history (*Mañana: Christian Theology from a Hispanic Perspective*. Nashville, TN: Abingdon, 1990). The inability to deal with ambiguity and sin led to a supposed destiny not manifest but infested with the demons of conquest and slavery.

Latinos and Latinas, the result of both Spanish and United States conquest, have long had to accept their ambiguous heritage. They are heirs to both saintly Spanish missionaries and rapacious conquerors, both Native American earth-wisdom and human sacrifice, both African slavery and bravery. It is the desire to hold all this tension in harmony that leads to the cosmic inclusiveness of art, music, and religious expression. The arrows of the ecstatic are flung from the bows of the aesthetic.

I have spent over twenty years guarding the sparks of ministerial experience and using the breath of personal reflection to coax them into the light of these *luminarias*. I now offer some practical advice to others who may not have had the privilege of bearing this tinder box.

Practical Pointers: A Rule of Dumb

"Ignorant" or "inexperienced" would admittedly be a better word than the common understanding of "dumb." But sometimes bumbling through a second language or bungling a sensitive cultural moment makes one feel dumb!

I will never be Mexican or Puerto Rican or Cuban. As I mentioned in the introduction, I value their histories and cultures. However, I need to explore what it means to be a white, middle-class, meat-eating, Midwestern male. God is with me too.

It is precisely through the blessing of these other communities that I have the distance actually to critique who I am, value that which is Gospel, and struggle to convert that which is only historical accident. It is this cultural distance, this perspective on myself and my society, which has been such a boon, and for which I am forever grateful to the Latinos and Latinas who have allowed me into their lives.

While I continue my personal struggle, however, I must strive at the very least to do no harm. Accepting the fact that I will never be an insider, I attempt to serve by adapting, evaluating, learning from my parishioners, and modifying my first impressions and inherent prejudgments. Some things I have learned from past mistakes include:

1. A methodological assumption that my parishioners' experience is as valuable as any book or seminary training.

I engage parishioners in a continual dialog with myself, their peers, and the Christian tradition in order to reflect together critically on this experience. Therefore, I do not evaluate a member's own beliefs, but rather encourage our ability to integrate this plurality.

2. An assumption that each person's context (culture, race, gender, etc.) has practical pedagogical applications. Therefore, with Hispanics, I:

a) Encourage cooperation rather than competition. Since they tend to be very family and community oriented, this approach builds on the strengths of their cultures.

b) Use appropriate physical and verbal reinforcement. What I may consider neutral behavior (e.g., rare expressions of approval) may be interpreted as coldness by this "high context" population.

c) Allow for a variety of evaluation techniques chosen by the community. This communicates a desire that we all succeed rather than an expectation that someone will be shamed. The question is not who is to blame, but what we can do to solve a common dilemma.

d) Seek to make explicit and immediate the practical consequences of theoretical concepts. Since there may be expectations that the authority figure (the pastor) be directive, this guidance helps people relate to and understand abstract ideas without compromising curiosity.

e) Consult widely with religious educators, always trying to include a menu of material from which people will find readings that both reinforce the validity of their experience yet challenge their interpretation of it.

f) Create an office and church environment that is respectful and friendly. I use decorations, music, snacks, etc., which make congregants feel at home.

g) Practice and encourage a hermeneutics of suspicion. Did United States Christianity begin with the thirteen colonies? Is popular piety always superstitious?

h) Be aware of and adapt to differences in cultural norms for decorum and discipline. For instance, if a Hispanic does not look the pastor in the eye, it may not be a result of guilt but an expression of respect.

i) Remember that some students learn better with circular rather than linear thinking. If a group values cooperative learning rather than competition between individuals, it may repeatedly return to previous themes until each member has grasped them even if that means not proceeding sequentially.

Conclusion

I continue to find cross-cultural ministry challenging. I still amaze myself at my ability to resist all my own best advice and lapse into previous, uncritical patterns. Indeed, it is a constant battle I may never win.

A first, unsuccessful coping strategy is what my colleagues term "trying to be more Hispanic than the Hispanics." This is impossible and unnecessary. It is impossible because I cannot be other than what God made me. It is unnecessary because love bridges otherness, it does not obliterate it. Thus I must treat myself as I hope to treat my parishioners, with care and patience, openness and wonderment, good-will and a willingness to learn good skills. This includes accepting the fact that I am still a gringo after all these years.

THE HISPANIC SHIFT: CONTINUITY
RATHER THAN CONVERSION?

Kenneth G. Davis, O.F.M., Conv.

This final chapter focuses on religious boundaries. Such borders may delineate denominations. However, there may be religious boundaries within the same denomination. I contend that the forces that are pushing Latinos and Latinas out of the Catholic Church and into others may be traced to tension within the Catholic communion, i.e., between popular and formal religion. I use the familiar outline of see, judge, act.

See

In 1989 the *New York Times* reported:

In a huge cultural transformation that is changing the face of religion in the United States, millions of Hispanic Americans have left the Roman Catholic Church for evangelical Protestant denominations.

This may be the most significant shift in religious affiliation since the Reformation, and represents a 20 percent loss of Catholic Hispanic membership in as many years. That is why the retired director of the Church's National Secretariat for Hispanic Affairs, Pablo Sedillo, questions whether there will be an identifiable United States Hispanic Catholic community within ten years. Such massive shifts in religious affiliation have ramifications far beyond Roman Catholicism. First, they will almost certainly affect the cultural identity of the various Hispanic subgroups. Second, other mainline churches must question the appeal of Pentecostalism to these and other minority communities. Indeed, growing fundamentalism has ramifications far beyond Christianity.

Moreover, there are many reasons to rue the squandering of five hundred years of Catholic evangelization among Hispanics. First, it is often caused by injustice and racism, which must be universally deplored and denounced. Second, it could very well spell the difference between flourishing life and only struggling survival, not only

117

for the Catholic Church but for other mainline United States Christian denominations. The late Joseph Fitzpatrick, S.J., contended that if we discounted Catholic immigrants, the church would be shrinking and aging at the same rate as mainline Protestant denominations. Are there not lessons here for all, perhaps especially those who see certain tenets and tactics of some Pentecostals as less than liberating? Lastly, as I have written elsewhere, I am convinced that understanding such a massive shift away from the church by any culture so historically permeated with Catholicism must be an important topic to anyone involved in religious studies. As environmentalists look to certain sensitive species as a litmus test for the health of the entire ecosystem, I argue that this massive shift in religious affiliation by Hispanics necessitates an investigation into our entire social, cultural, political, and economic "ecosystem"; what is the appeal of Pentecostalism, and the consequences of such a massive shift in religious affiliation? I propose a new framework for this investigation, drawing on my own discipline, which is pastoral theology.

One of the fastest-growing Hispanic denominations is Pentecostalism, a term as amorphous as "Hispanic." By Pentecostal I mean those organized religions such as Assemblies of God, and those unorganized or independent groups, which share the following beliefs: (1) salvation is based solely on a personal relationship with Jesus Christ; (2) one's reaction to such a relationship necessarily results in the transformation of one's life and an outpouring of the gifts of the Holy Spirit, especially healings and tongues; (3) the Bible is the sole religious and historical authority; (4) Christians must act on the "Great Commission" to bring all people to accept Jesus as their savior.

These beliefs, intimately related to the prevalent Anglo-American ethos of individualism, are decidedly anti-elitist or populist. Hence the poor and marginated are often attracted and offered a simple (fundamental) doctrine.

Judge

Why have one million United States Catholic Hispanics left for Pentecostal and other denominations in the last thirty years? I posit that we may not be witnessing so much a shift of institutional loyalties as an evolution in the centuries-old conflict between official Catholic, and Hispanic popular, religion. I further opine that the *sensus fidelium* (sense of the faithful) preserved in that same Hispanic popular religion is a necessary and healthy balance to the Anglo-American ideological domination of all United States Christian churches.

By popular religion I mean the Hispanic cultures' underlying beliefs about God expressed in a complex of domestic devotions and expressions of the Divinity. There are important points which distinguish (without dichotomizing) popular from official religion. First, the symbol system of popular religion is controlled by the laity, especially the marginated. The grandmother (or other women) is often the priestess of these rituals rather than the clergy. She maintains the home altar and coordinates the prayers, candles, and flowers offered there. Contradicting prevalent prejudice, Ada María Isasi-Díaz, Ana María Díaz-Stevens, and others have shown how women enjoy great power and autonomy in Hispanic communities precisely as the guardians of popular religiosity. Second, popular religion is intrinsically petitionary. The daily necessities and struggles of life are unabashedly, even insistently, manifested to God and God's representatives. Therefore people gather in their homes to pray novenas and rosaries confident of miracles like those attested to in the lives of the saints. Third, there is a strong sense that martyrdom, or suffering solidarity, is an essential part of the spiritual life. Bloody crucifixes and suffering Virgins are at the center of contemplation. When Hispanics reenact the way of the cross in their streets, it is because they know that Jesus suffers in solidarity with them in their homes and barrios. Fourth, popular religion is based on a pre-Enlightenment worldview. Community rather than individualism is appreciated, affective rather than cognitive appropriation of religion is valued, ardor reigns over order. That is a reason why celebrations begin not when some mechanical god chimes, but rather when the people are assembled and ready to pray to a God who is in personal solidarity with them.

Since Trent, official Catholic religion has been more uniform, abstract, and bureaucratic. Therefore, it has often conflicted with this popular vestige of its own medieval past. Official religion has tried alternately to proscribe, prescribe, or tolerate popular religion. A famous example of this was the persecution of the *penitentes*, a Hispanic confraternity concentrated in New Mexico. For self-protection the confraternity observed great secrecy, and jealously guarded its places of worship. Even today, after reconciliatory documents such as *Evangelii Nuntiandi*, officials of the church often only deign to treat popular religion as the object of analysis, rather than as the subject of spirituality. Popular religion has responded sometimes with submission, or, when pressed, with anticlericalism. Mostly though, popular religion has existed in an uneasy parallel with official religion. People practice their daily domestic faith and on the occasion of some popular ritual controlled by the clergy (e.g., baptism) they go to church.

This clash has a long and complicated history. The Spanish missionaries arrived in the Americas before Trent. It was popular religion (then in a more dialectic relationship with official religion) which they taught to the people. At the time this was pastorally wise because the clergy necessary to official religion were too few. To this day popular religion is the prime catechesis of the Hispanic household. See the chapter by Jaime Lara in the book I edited, *Misa, Mesa, y Musa: Liturgy in the United States Hispanic Church* (Schiller Park, IL: J.S. Paluch, 1997).

The Enlightenment, the Reformation, and modernity all created a reaction in official Catholic religion. In the United States, this process was accelerated by the Americanization of the church. When in 1848 the United States government conquered first what is now the western half of the country (formerly Mexico), and fifty years later Puerto Rico, the United States Church which entered those lands was in many ways a civil religion. The church usually failed to defend the rights of Hispanics under treaties with the United States government, native clergy were alienated (e.g., the seminary at Taos, New Mexico, was closed), and Hispanic popular religion was judged to be at best anachronistic, at worst superstitious. This is not to reject the (necessarily) institutional church, or to ignore the many unknown prophets who valiantly served the poor. It is simply to acknowledge the painful fact that generally the church which entered those conquered lands shared the worldview of the conqueror, and felt it had to evangelize and convert its inhabitants. This, of course, means they were unaware of, or attached little importance to, the mainly popular Catholic religion which had arrived there before the founding of Jamestown.

Around 1968 the conquered people began to publicly claim the value of their own cultural expressions of religion. Many Hispanic thinkers today defend and encourage popular religion as both the most pristine expression of the United States Hispanic cultures, and the historic guardian of those cultures in the face of political and ecclesial discrimination. Thus Ana María Díaz Stevens and Anthony M. Stevens-Arroyo, while contesting the history outlined above, agree with this conclusion (*Recognizing the Latino Resurgence in United States Religion: The Emmaus Paradigm.* Boulder, CO: Westview Press, 1998).

Only now are church officials beginning to appreciate (and dialogue with) this most ancient expression of Christianity in America. I posit that many of its practitioners may have already found other expressions of popular religion (within the Catholic Church this includes movements such as the charismatics), for example, the move toward Pentecostalism. Further, that religion ought to be analyzed as an evolution in this struggle between popular and official Catholicism, rather than as a denominational contest. Note the parallels between Pentecostalism and the dynamics of popular religion. In the Pentecostal Church the symbol system is controlled by the laity. People freely use oil, water, and the laying on of hands in their confident efforts to win divine favors for themselves and others. Most importantly, however, the primordial symbol of the community—Scripture—is equally accessible to everyone. The Bible is not a book of the elite who mediates its message through the esoteric study of hermeneutics and exegesis. Rather it is immediately accessible to anyone who has a personal relationship to its framer, Jesus Christ. Consequently, the laity support the church economically, sometimes directly control it through trusteeship, and are not averse to beginning another church if they disagree with the pastor. And the pastor is often not much different (in terms of culture, socioeconomic position, education, occupation, marital status) than the people. Both meaning-making (through symbols) and decision-making are shared widely by the entire church.

These churches often emphasize the immediate economic and physical gains of faith: "name it and claim it" expresses the importance petitionary prayer holds. In Catholic popular religiosity people erect plaques to make personal testimony in public, liturgical space; among Pentecostals, personal testimony in public liturgy is an essential and emotional part of virtually every liturgy.

While stressing such aspects of modernity as individualism, the idea of the mutual aid is promoted. Therefore the congregation as a whole, or the pastor personally, cares for members who are experiencing emotional, financial, or spiritual need. However, individualism remains the underlying anthropology: church membership is not a result of culture and history but rather an individual decision. Since the person is not valued as an essentially social creature, community is only a voluntary, temporary, negotiable relationship between isolated individuals. While this relationship is often experienced as affective and useful, it is not understood as mediating the faith; it is utilitarian and dispensable. Hence the Pentecostal penchant for splintering.

Lastly, the spirituality of martyrdom evolves into a strong appreciation of the apocalypse. Just as the coming of the Messiah was the hope of the downtrodden of Israel, so the second coming is the salve for all the wounds a poor, marginated Hispanic suffers. God is not so much seen as a crucified victim who suffers with the people, but rather as a warrior who will ultimately justify the righteous. Neither the spirituality of martyrdom (suffering with Jesus as a share in his holiness) nor that of the apocalypse (sharing Jesus' victory in the next life) changes those social structures which afflict the Hispanic. But the latter is an evolution of the former insofar as it continues to give religious meaning to the suffering of the people.

I suggest therefore that the dynamics of Catholic popular religion and those of Pentecostalism are strikingly similar. Perhaps the exodus of Hispanic Catholics has more to do with the unfortunate lack of a dialogue between popular and official Catholic religion, and less to do with institutional loyalties and denominational competition. If for centuries official representatives of Catholicism have snubbed the traditional piety of Latinos and Latinas, and if for the first time in centuries that church no longer has either a legal or social monopoly on Hispanics, and if the ancient intuitions expressed by that piety evolve in the postmodern world in such a way that they can still be expressed within another Christian body, can "proselytism by sects" be the only reason the United States Catholic Church is losing its most ancient ethnic ally?

Pentecostalism may represent a perceived resource for the psychological, cultural, and social survival of a Hispanic who experiences both dominant society and church authority as a threat to that survival. Perhaps the absolute certainty offered in these barrio churches is a greater defense against the risk and ambiguity which confronts the poor of modern society than the "cultural coldness, the systematized, privileged, and secularized Christendom of North

America" (Read, W.R. *Brazil 1980*. Moravia, CA: Mission Advanced Research and Communication Center, 1973).

If there is some truth in this hypothesis, then the call by Hispanic Catholic leadership to recognize popular religion as both a subject of spirituality for the whole church and the object of a specifically Hispanic theology is even more credible. Therefore any analysis of this enormous shift in religious affiliation must see the similarity and evolution involved, and not become lost in denominational dithering. The traditional churches may indeed provide the unity, historical continuity, and universality necessary to balance and correct popular religion while Pentecostalism may not. However, the fundamental error has been to blithely correct without wanting to be corrected. Numerous volumes, hundreds of articles, thousands of homilies have been written about how this religiosity can be accommodated in official liturgies, corrected by insights of social justice, nuanced by an appreciation of history. All of this is true. But where is it written, preached, taught that popular religion can add drama to routinized liturgy, warmth to segregated communities, and passion to domesticated theology? Popular religion provides an urgently needed balance to the cerebral, bureaucratic, xenophobic tendencies of mainline United States Christianity. The personal experience of community, the emotive nature of conversion, the felt need of a marginated community to assault the heavens with petitions, the somatic experience of the crucified Christ through institutionalized martyrdom, all need to be commemorated by the symbols of the people in the hands of the people. There is no necessary conflict between official and popular religion; rather there is historic continuity and dialectic possibilities. An analytic framework based on this appreciation would be useful.

We still do not know the full consequence of the Hispanic exodus. Will their Catholic culture influence Pentecostalism? Or will they rather lose their own cultural identity within that modern, historically Anglophone milieu? This chapter simply points out boundaries and suggests bridges; it is too brief to begin their actual construction. However, I am convinced of one thing. The mainline churches in the United States will be spiritually poorer (and also numerically smaller and older) if they squander this opportunity to retrieve those ancient, vibrant intuitions so often preserved by our Hispanic sisters and brothers.

Act

The original essay on which this chapter is based was well received. I make bold therefore to again include a few suggestions from my own discipline on how to facilitate a dialogue between Hispanic popular and mainline United States religions. I conclude with suggestions for research by other disciplines based on the analytic framework outlined above.

First, recognize the importance of dialogue with feminists. Women have been in the forefront of both pastoral care and theological enterprise among United States Hispanics. This might be because pastoral care in popular religion usually devolved on women and often empowered them. Consequently, reflection on it has been the theological focus of United States Hispanic theology. It is distinguished from Latin American theology by, among other things, the early and continued contribution of women. Similarly, anthropologist Margarita Melville has stated that Hispanic feminists from the secular disciplines have been less stridently condemnatory of religion than their male counterparts, perhaps because they have found autonomy, meaning, and power in Christian rituals. Witness what Greek Orthodox artist Cristina Emmanuel of Puerto Rico says:

> The images I use . . . the Virgins and saints are part of my own empowerment and are not isolated in traditional associations. They are remythologized. (For example) Santa Cristina is not a martyr but a warrior and the Madre Dolorosa's suffering is a transformation, an opening of the heartspace. (Mesa-Bains, Amalia, ed. *Ceremony of Memory: New Expressions in Spirituality Among Contemporary Hispanic Artists*. Santa Fe, NM: Center for Contemporary Arts of Santa Fe, 1988)

Does not something similar happen as well in Santería? Rosendo Urrabazo and others have much to say about Anglo prejudices concerning "machismo" and other aspects of the Hispanic culture, and Robert Goizueta has explored how feminism can challenge the romanticization of Hispanic cultures.

Second, dialogue about social justice. Popular religiosity contains the seed of true Hispanic liberation. Not only has it maintained those cultures in the face of centuries of imperialism, it sometimes explodes into liberating action. It is no accident that the United Farm Workers march and strike under a banner of Our Lady of Guadalupe. Certain approaches to liberation theology can alarm some Hispanics because the church has a checkered history in its involvement with Latin American politics. Casting liberation talk into the meaning-making system of popular religion may make it more acceptable, effective, and powerful.

Third, dialogue with the complexity of Hispanic families. The hierarchy and mutuality of popular religion (with respect to saints, angels, and Mary) express similar dynamics extant in the Hispanic family. The family (like the Catholic Church and Christianity itself) can deteriorate due to such aspects of modernity as consumerism, secularism, individualism, and rationalism. If the Hispanic culture does not produce material wealth, foster a relativistic morality, promote libertine individuality, or admit empiricism as the only arbiter of reality, then it will conflict with much of United States society and experience internal or external anomie (literally "lawlessness"). However, when an institution as powerful and respected as the church encourages and animates (i.e., is in dialectic relation with) popular religion, especially when it includes the whole family, then much of this cognitive dissonance is eased. By making explicit what is implicit in popular religion (e.g., a personal commitment to the justice of Christ), by helping people become conscious of what is rooted in their collective unconscious (the human person is social creature), by celebrating solidarity with God and continuity of culture (elucidated in Scripture), the Christian Church in effect will mediate new meaning, retrieved from popular religion, which will respond constructively to urbanized, modern realities. Moreover, it will respond with strategies of proven effectiveness: (1) indigenous leadership leading (popular) rituals; (2) indigenous financing (e.g., through confraternities) for such rituals; (3) a widespread sense of belonging to and responsibility toward the community; in popular religion everyone participates. Such a dialectic will also help the whole of church and society experience Hispanic communities as not a marginal problem but a source of richness.

Lastly, since socioeconomic discrimination and racism are sadly a sinful presence in our communities, perhaps the rites of popular religion can begin to create real *inter*cultural dialogue, resulting in *intra*cultural analysis, rather than multicultural meltdown. This is especially true with the rites of Hispanic popular religion which contain elements of European, Native American, and African religions. That is why Latinos have been called the "cosmic race."

Conclusion

Hispanics are shifting religious affiliation in numbers unknown since the fifteenth century. Too often members of various churches have seen this as a question of denominational competition. It may be more accurate to view this phenomenon as one battle in the long war between official and popular Catholicism. Certainly it raises questions for all Christians and others interested in the study of religion.

Sociologists need to ask why this occurs. Is it due mainly to shifts from rural to urban zones, from pre-modern to post-modern world-views, and the resulting cultural anomie? This seems to be the opinion of Joseph Fitzpatrick. However, his colleague, Allan Deck, S.J., seems to find more fault with the institutions of the church. And once Hispanics join another religion, do they remain loyal to it, or do they begin to commit to a series of denominations?

Anthropologists must question how this shift from five hundred years of Catholicism affects the Hispanic cultures, and how it does or will influence the culture of Pentecostal churches.

Political scientists might inquire about a shift from those denominations which more explicitly support liberation efforts to those which do not affect Latinos.

From the perspective of pastoral theology, I offer the theory that this shift is not so much about denominational loyalty but rather psychological, cultural, and social survival of the United States' oldest expression of Christianity. Failure to dialogue with this past in our present will deprive all United States Christians of an urgent and necessary balance and corrective, and certainly has unknown consequences for all Hispanics. Neither usurpation nor conversion, this is an active invitation to a mutually beneficial dialectic, a call to retrieve continuity with our own past. Any Christian, indeed any person of goodwill, must be concerned about changes in

> . . . the culture of Spanish America (which) also brings its own gifts. When asked, both new immigrants and long-established Hispanic Americans speak of religion—not only Catholicism, but something more like a deep sense of the

sacred, a recognition that the world is holy, which is probably the oldest and deepest certitude of the Amerindian world. (Fuentes, Carlos. *The Buried Mirror: Reflections on Spain in the New World*. New York, NY: Houghton, Miflin Company, 1992)

CONCLUSION

Yolanda Tarango, C.C.V.I.

The desire to be a church, "which is in truth universal," is expressed by the United States Bishops in their *Pastoral Letter on Hispanic Ministry*. They describe "a Church with open arms, welcoming different gifts and expressions of our 'one Lord, one faith, one baptism, one God and father of all.' (Eph. 4:5–6)." Latino Catholics in the United States continually re-echo this invitation to prophetic pluralism. The chapters in this volume add still another chorus articulating the historic longing for a truly universal church where all can feel at home. To be a universal church is to be both one, united in faith, and different, reflective of the many expressions of that same faith. A review of the literature on Hispanic ministry in the last twenty-five years indicates that the Latina/o community in the United States still does not experience the universality that their church professes to witness. Latina/os in the United States are still striving to find their place around the common table. The search for inclusion is implicit in the consistent and resounding call for recognition of the Latina/o contribution to the tradition and theology of the Catholic Church.

The last three decades have seen a concerted effort on the part of Latina/o Catholics to claim our place within the identity of the United States Catholic Church. Seeking our identity as full members within the United States Catholic Church means that we cannot be limited to being objects of the church's ministry. We see ourselves as participants in our church's ministry. We expect to be part of setting the norm for what it means to be a Catholic in the United States, and we want our cultural/ethnic religious understandings and practices to be valued and reflected as part of the identity of our church.

Since Vatican II, Latina/os in the United States Catholic Church have emerged from a position of invisibility. Spurred by the civil rights movement, we discovered our public voice in a common identity as Latina/os, and used it to draw attention to the lack of appropriate pastoral services in our communities. The church's pastoral ministry at the time could best be characterized as "one size fits all." Factors such as language, culturally significant celebrations,

129

and the historical traditions of diverse communities were not taken into account. Furthermore, the church's participation in Americanization efforts helped to shape an assimilationist approach to pastoral ministry that disregarded contributions by groups outside of the dominant culture. Even though Latina/os were the first Catholics in the United States, we were expected to assimilate into the "American" church and leave our culturally inspired beliefs and practices at the door in exchange for a generic set of beliefs that would allow us to "fit in."

For the past twenty years, as in this volume, we have been telling our story, both to underscore the complexity and diversity of the Latina/o community in the United States, and to say that we come to the church with all of who we are: our history, traditions, and religious practices. Our differences can enrich the church and bolster its catholicity. Unfortunately, however, we have often been treated as a large pastoral problem. This stems from the false assumption that Latina/os have little to contribute and are principally recipients of the church's pastoral care. This perception is acknowledged by the bishops in their *Pastoral Letter on Hispanic Ministry*, when they emphasize that the Hispanic community in the United States is not a problem to be solved but a blessing from God. The gift that Latina/os bear is a call to the church to a universality where "each finds a place and all feel welcome."

The distinguishing mark of a universal church is its capacity to embrace all the differences that exist among its members without viewing some as superior to others. The challenge to universality is not the existence of differences, but the ordering of differences that gives some greater value than others, thus allowing a dominant trend to develop. When this happens a norm is set which defines and limits what it means, for example, to be Catholic in the United States Those who are different are forced to repress or hide their differences in order to fit into the established norm. Latina/os in the United States are attempting to break that norm and the boundaries that have limited our full inclusion in the United States Catholic Church by insisting on being accepted with all of our differences. Only then can we consider ourselves as fully accepted. Inclusion in the church is not about being counted in the census or filling the pews or having more culturally sensitive pastoral care delivered. It means being able to give and receive from the full authenticity of who we are. We highlight the differences because they distinguish who we are and what we have to offer. If our contribution is truly embraced and valued, we become participants in shaping the norm for United States Catholicism.

The chapters in this volume represent the continuing call to the church's true, universal identity since each focuses on a different Latina/o group. They also suggest pastoral approaches that may be appropriate to a universal church. An important issue for Latina/os in the Unied States is that we not be viewed as a uni-dimensional, homogenized group. We value and recognize the differences among ourselves, and want to make them known. This collection is an attempt to highlight different groups that form the Latino community in the United States. We have placed particular emphasis on those groups that are least well known.

As Latina/os we have in common the Spanish language, a history of conquest, and with that the Catholic tradition. However, our histories, cultures, and even native cuisine are different for each group. Therefore, there is no single pastoral strategy that will be appropriate for all Latina/os. Nor will pastoral approaches imported from Central or Latin America be adequate.

The following four principles, gleaned from the writings in this collection, might serve as touchstones in the development of a pastoral plan for Latina/os in a universal church.

Valuing differences: In order to truly value differences we must engage them and let them change us. It is not enough to appreciate differences from a distance. We need pastoral strategies that allow people to experience and engage each other's differences in order to promote understanding between people of different cultures and among Latina/os of different cultures and classes.

Positive cultural identity: Fostering a positive cultural self-identity for Latina/os in the United States is critical because the dominant culture has historically devalued Latino culture. Young Latina/os especially must have a strong, positive cultural identity because they are living between cultures.

Dignity of persons: Promoting human dignity is a Gospel mandate reinforced by the preferential option for the poor that calls for promoting the dignity especially of the poor and marginalized. Latina/os in United States culture are in large part poor and marginalized.

Mutuality in ministry: The ability to give and to receive is empowering and, for Latina/os in the church, a symbol of true belonging. Being treated as objects of ministry, because we are not thought of as having anything to offer, has often disempowered Latina/os in the church. We need pastoral strategies that promote and encourage Latina/os' active participation in the church's ministry.

In conclusion, only mutual respect and love will lead us to become the universal church we strive for. Our hope is that this book will further the reflection and take us one step closer to being a truly Catholic Church.

SUPPLEMENTAL BIBLIOGRAPHY

"Original Fervor": A New Catholic Reformation?

Azevedo, S.J., Marcello. "Hispanic Leaders: Faith and Culture in the New Millennium." *Chicago Studies* 36 (December 1997), 224–242.

Davis, Kenneth G. "A Return to the Roots: Conversion and the Culture of Mexican-Descent Catholics." *Pastoral Psychology* 40 (3) January 1992: 139–158.

Deck, Allan Figueroa, S.J. "Latino Religion and the Struggle for Justice: Evangelization as Conversion." *Journal of Hispanic/Latino Theology* 4 (3) February 1997: 28–41.

Doyle, Ruth T. & Scarpetta, Olga, eds. *La Formación y el Ministerio: Preparación Para un Ministerio que Favorezca El Desarrollo del Liderazgo Hispano*. New York, NY: Office of Pastoral Research and Planning, Archdiocese of New York, 1989.

Espín, Orlando O. "Pentecostalism and Popular Catholicism: The Poor and *Tradition*" *Journal of Hispanic/Latino Theology* 3 (2) November 1995: 14–43.

Goizueta, Roberto S. "The Church and Hispanics in the United States: From Empowerment to Solidarity." In *That They Might Live*, M. Downey, ed. New York, NY: Crossroad, 1991.

National Conference of Catholic Bishops. *The Hispanic Presence, Challenge, and Commitment: A Pastoral Letter on Hispanic Ministry, December 12, 1983*. Washington, DC: United States Catholic Conference, 1984.

Pastoral Care of Catholic South Americans Living in the United States

Casarela, Peter. "The Painted Word." Journal of Hispanic/Latino Theology. 6 (2) November 1998: 18–42.

García Rivera, Alejandro. *St. Martin de Porres: The "Little Stories" and the Semiotics of Culture*. Maryknoll, NY: Orbis Books, 1995.

Nida, Eugene A. *Understanding Latin Americans: With Special Reference to Religious Values and Movements*. South Pasadena, CA: William Carey Library, 1974.

Romero, Gilbert C. *Hispanic Devotional Piety: Tracing the Biblical Roots*. Maryknoll, NY: Orbis Books, 1991.

Challenges to the Pastoral Care of Central Americans in the United States

Bachelis, Faren. *The Central Americans*. New York, NY: Chelsea House Publishers, 1990.

Bau, Ignatius. *This Ground Is Holy: Church Sanctuary and Central American Refugees*. Mahwah, NJ: Paulist Press, 1985.

Crittenden, Ann. *Sanctuary: A Story of American Conscience and Law in Collision*. New York, NY: Weidenfeld and Nicolson, 1988.

Fitzpatrick, Joseph P. "No Place to Grieve." *America* 163 (21 July, 1990): 37–38.

Henríquez, José luis. "Pobreza Principal Problema de C.A." *La Prensa Gráfica* (El Salvador), (27 July, 1999): 30.

Menjívar, Cecilia. "Immigrant Social Networks: Implications and Lessons for Policy." *Harvard Journal of Hispanic Policy* 8 (1994–1995): 35–58.

Smith, Christian. *Resisting Reagan: The United States Central American Peace Movement*. Chicago, IL: The University of Chicago Press, 1996.

Wellmeier, Nancy J. "Santa Eulalia's People in Exile: Maya Religion, Culture, and Identity in Los Angeles." R.S. Warner and J.G. Wittner, eds., *Gathering in Diaspora: Religious Communities and the New Immigration.* Philadelphia, PA: Temple University Press, 1988.

Wilbanks, Dana W. "The Sanctuary Movement and United States Refugee Policy: A Paradigm for Christian Public Ethics." *Theology and Public Policy* 6 (2) Winter 1994: 4–18.

Dominican Immigrants: Social and Religious Context

Bahn, Adele & Angela Jaquez. "One Style of Dominican Bridal Shower." in Boggs, Vernon, etal., eds. *The Apple Sliced: Sociological Studies of New York City.* NYC: Praeger, 1984.

Doyle, Ruth T. & Scarpetta, Olga, eds. "Social Relations Within the Family in the Dominican Republic and United States: Continuity and Change." In *Hispanics in New York: Religious, Cultural and Social Experiences.* New York, NY: Office of Pastoral Research and Planning, Archdiocese of New York, 1989.

Dwyer, Christopher. *The Dominican Americans.* New York, NY: Chelsea House Publishers, 1991.

Falcon, Luis M. *Features of the Hispanic Underclass: Puerto Ricans and Dominicans in New York City.* Ithaca, NY: Dept. of Sociology, New York State College of Agriculture and Life Sciences, 1990.

Kathryn, Wolford. "From American Dreams to Dominican Hope." *Christian Century* 107 (May 1990): 1137–1139.

Levitt, Peggy. "Local-Level Global Religion: The Case of United States Dominican Migration." *Journal for the Scientific Study of Religion* 37 (1) 1998: 74–89.

Paulino, Ana M. "Death, Dying, and Religion Among Dominican Immigrants." In *A Cross-Cultural Look at Death, Dying, and Religion.* Joan K. Parry & Angela Shen Ryan, eds. Chicago, IL: Nelson-Hall Publishers, 1995.

Torres-Saillant, Silvio & Hernandez, Ramona. *The Dominican Americans*. Greenwood Publishing Group, 1998.

Pastoral Care of "*Los Marielitos*"

Brandon, George. *Santeria from Africa to the New World: The Dead Sell Memories*. Indianapolis, IN: Indiana University Press, 1997.

Olson, James & Judith E. *Cuban Americans: From Trauma to Triumph*. New York, NY: Twayne Publishers, 1995.

Roman, Augustin A. "Cuban Ecclesial Reflection Communities in the Diaspora." *Migration World Magazine* 21 (1993): 27–29.

The Pastoral Care of the Puerto Rican Woman in the United States

Díaz-Stevens, Ana María. *Oxcart Catholicism on Fifth Avenue: The Impact of the Puerto Rican Migration Upon the Archdiocese of New York*. Notre Dame, IN: University of Notre Dame Press, 1993.

_____."The Saving Grace: The Matriarchal Core of Latino Catholicism." *Latino Studies Journal* 4 (September, 1993): 60–78.

Isasi-Diaz, Ada Maria. *Mujerista Theology: A Theology for the Twenty-First Century*. Maryknoll, NY: Orbis Books, 1996.

Isolina Ferré, María. *In Quest of a Vision: Sister Isolina's Own Story of Gospel Servanthood Among Puerto Ricans*. Mahwah, NJ: Paulist Press, 1997.

Sanchez, Franklyn D. "Puerto Rican Spiritualism: Survival of the Spirit." In *Historical Perspectives on Puerto Rican Survival in the United States*. Princeton, NJ: Markus Wiener Publishers, 1980.

Sanchez-Korrol, Virginia. "Between Two Worlds: Educated Puerto Rican Migrant Women." *Caribbean Review* 12 (Summer 1983): 26–29.

Sotomayor, Marta, ed. *In Triple Jeopardy—Aged Hispanic Women:*

Insights and Experiences. Washington, DC: National Hispanic Council, 1994.

Stevens-Arroyo, Antonio M., ed. *Prophets Denied Honor: An Anthology on the Hispano Church of the United States.* Maryknoll, NY: Orbis Books, 1980.

_____."Puerto Rican Struggles in the Catholic Church." In *Historical Perspectives on Puerto Rican Survival in the United States.* Princeton, NJ: Markus Wiener Publishers, 1980.

Seven Tips on the Pastoral Care of United States Catholics of Mexican Descent

Doyle, Ruth T. & Scarpetta, Olga (eds.). "Significant Elements Which May Affect the Adjustment of Hispanics to American Culture." In *Hispanics in New York: Religious, Cultural and Social Experiences,* second edition. New York, NY: Office of Pastoral Research and Planning, Archdiocese of New York, 1989.

Elizondo, Virgilio. "A Theological Interpretation of the Mexican-American Experience." In *Christianity and Culture: An Introduction to Pastoral Theology and Ministry for Bicultural Community.* Huntington, IN: Our Sunday Visitor, Inc., 1975.

Gonzalez, Roberto A. & Velle, Michaella. *The Hispanic in the United States: A Sociological and Religious Profile.* New York, NY: Northeast Catholic Pastoral Center for Hispanics, 1985.

Hemrick, Eugene F. (ed). *Strangers and Aliens No Longer, Part I: The Hispanic Presence in the Church of the United States.* Washington, DC: United States Catholic Conference, 1993.

Hurtado, Juan. "An Attitudinal Study of Social Distance Between the Mexican American and the Church." In *Prophets Denied Honor: An Anthology on the Hispano Church of the United States.* Antonio M. Stevens Arroyo, ed., Maryknoll: NY Orbis Books, 1980.

Lampe, Philip E. "The Practice of Religion Among Hispanics." In

Hispanics in the Church. Philip E. Lampe, ed. San Francisco, CA: Catholic Scholars Press, 1993.

Rodriguez, Jeannette. *Our Lady of Guadalupe: Faith and Empowerment.* Austin, TX: Austin University of Texas, 1994.

Thies, Jeffrey, S. *Mexican Catholicism in Southern California: The Importance of Popular Religiosity and Sacramental Practices in Faith.* New York, NY: Peter Lang, 1993.

Hispanic Catholic Youth in the United States

Anderson, G. "Two Igantian Anniversaries on New York's Lower East Side." *America* 163 (Oct. 1990): 223–225.

Carrasquillo, Angela. *Hispanic Children and Youth in the United States: A Resource Guide.* New York, NY: Garland Publications, 1991.

Cervantes, Carmen Maria. "Youth and Evangelization." In *Perspectivas: Hispanic Ministry.* Allan Deck et al., eds. Kansas City, MO: Sheed & Ward, 1995.

DeBalssie, Adele M. DeBlassie, Richard R. "Education of Hispanic Youth: A Cultural Lag." *Adolescence* 31 (Spring 1996): 205–217.

DeBalssie, Richard R. *Counseling with Mexican American Youth: Preconceptions and Processes.* Austin, TX: Learning Concepts, 1976.

Diaz-Stevens, Ana Maria & Stevens-Arroyo, Anthony. Recognizing the Latino Resurgence in United States Religion: The Emmaus Paradigm. Boulder, CO: Westview Press, 1998.

Doyle, Ruth T. & Scarpetta, Olga (eds.). "Formación y el Ministerio: Preparación Para un Ministerio Juvenil." In *Hispanics in New York: Religious, Cultural, and Social Experiences.* New York, NY: Office of Pastoral Research and Planning, Archdiocese of New York, 1989.

Prophets of Hope Editorial Team. *Evangelization of Hispanic Young People*. Winona, MN: Saint Mary's Press, 1995.

_____. *Hispanic Young People and the Church's Pastoral Response*. Winona, MN: St. Mary's Press, 1994.

Ramirez, Margaret. "The Gangs and Their God." *Los Angeles Times* (8 May, 1999): Metro; Part B; page two.

Secretariat for Hispanic Affairs. *Prophetic Voices: The Document on the Process of the III Encuentro Nacional Hispano de Pastoral*. Washington, DC: United States Catholic Conference, 1986.

Still Gringo After All These Years: The Minister in a Cross-Cultural Context

Davis, Kenneth G. "On Being a Frog in my Field," *The Priest* 47 (10): October 1991: 6–7.

_____."Preaching in Spanish as a Second Language." In Allan Deck, S.J., et al., eds. *Perspectivas*. Kansas City, MO: Sheed and Ward, 1995.

_____."Presiding in Spanish as a Second Language," In Davis, Kenneth G., ed. *Misa, Mesa y Musa*. Schiller Park, IL: The J.S. Paluch Co., 1997.

Folliard, Dorothy, O.P. "MACC as Graced Whirlpool: Some Reflections from a Non-Hispanic." *Listening* 32 (3) Fall 1997: 179–187.

Garzon, Fernando & Ltan, Siang-Yang. "Counseling Hispanics: Cross-Cultural and Christian Perspectives." *Journal of Psychology and Christianity* 11 (Winter 1992): 378–390.

Lampe, Philip E. "Is the Church Meeting the Needs of Hispanics?" *Living Light* 27 (1) Fall 1990: 51–55.

Long, Daniel M. "Toward Effective Ministry with Hispanics." *Word and World* 5 (Winter, 1985): 33–42.

Rubio, José Antonio. "Checklist for Multicultural and Multilingual Worship." *Liturgy* 14 (4) 1998: 23–26.

The Hispanic Shift: Continuity Rather Than Conversion?

Cornelius, Hughes. "Views from the Pews: Hispanic and Anglo Catholics in a Changing Church." *Review of Religious Research* 33 (4) June 1992: 364–375.

Markides, Kyriakos S. "Change and Continuity in Mexican American Religious Behavior: A Three-Generation Study." In *The Mexican American Experience: An Interdisciplinary Anthology.* Rodolfo O. de la Garza et al., ed. Austin, TX: University of Texas Press, Austin, 1985.

Leon, Luis. "Born Again in East L.A.: The Congregation as Border Space." R.S. Warner and J.G. Wittner, eds., *Gathering in Diaspora: Religious Communities and the New Immigration.* Philadelphia, PA: Temple University Press, 1988.

Ramírez, Ricardo. "The Crisis in Ecumenism Among Hispanic Christians." *Origins* 24 (40) March 1995: 660–667.

Robeck, Cecil M., Jr. "Evangelization or Proselytism of Hispanics? A Pentecostal Perspective." *Journal of Hispanic/Latino Theology* 4 (4) May 1997: 42–64.

CONTRIBUTORS

George Boran does leadership training for youth throughout Latin America and is a visiting lecturer at Fordham University in the Bronx.

Irma S. Corretjer-Nolla served as Outreach Project Director for the Mexican American Cultural Center in San Antonio, TX.

Kenneth G. Davis is an award-winning author and editor. He coordinates Hispanic ministry formation at St. Meinrad School of Theology in St. Meinrad, Indiana.

Eduardo C. Fernández is an adjunct professor of pastoral theology at the Jesuit School of Theology in Berkeley, California.

Adele J. González is the assistant director of the Office of Lay Ministry for the Archdiocese of Miami, Florida.

Anneris Goris is an associate director of RISC—a national survey of Latino parishes and congregations at Brooklyn College, City University of New York.

Ada María Isasi-Díaz, born and raised in La Habana, Cuba, works developing a Mujerista Theology, a Hispanic women liberation theology. She resides in New York City.

Fanny Tabares is the regional coordinator of Hispanic pastoral care in the diocese of Grand Rapids, Michigan.

Yolanda Tarango teaches in the Religious Studies Department of the University of the Incarnate Word and is the director of the Visitation House Transitional Housing Project in San Antonio, Texas.

INDEX